ADDICTS
AND ADDICTIONS

Other books by Vernon Coleman

On Medicine
The Medicine Men
Paper Doctors
Everything you want to know about Ageing
Stress Control
The Home Pharmacy
Face Values
Aspirin or Ambulance
Guilt
Stress and your Stomach
A Guide to Child Health
An A–Z of Women's Problems
The Good Medicine Guide
Bodypower
Bodysense
Taking Care of Your Skin
Life Without Tranquillisers
Eczema and Dermatitis
High Blood Pressure
Arthritis
Diabetes
The Story of Medicine

On Cricket
Thomas Winsden's Cricketing Almanack
Diary of A Cricket Lover

As Edward Vernon
Practice Makes Perfect
Practise What You Preach
Getting Into Practice
Aphrodisiacs: An Owner's Manual
Aphrodisiacs: An Owner's Manual: Bumper Omnibus Edition
The Complete Guide to Life

As Marc Charbonnier
Tunnel

ADDICTS AND ADDICTIONS

Dr Vernon Coleman

PIATKUS

© 1986 Vernon Coleman
First published in 1986 by
Judy Piatkus (Publishers) Limited, London

British Library Cataloguing in Publication Data

Coleman, Vernon
    Addicts and addictions.
    1. Drug abuse
    I. Title
    616.86   RC564

    ISBN 0–86188–371–3

Edited by Margaret Daykin
Designed by Paul Saunders

Typeset by Phoenix Photosetting, Chatham
Printed and bound at The Bath Press, Avon

CONTENTS

CHAPTER

1

THE 20ᵀᴴ CENTURY PLAGUE

Addiction is now a world-wide problem. There are millions of addicts in every major developed country in the Western world. Addictions wreck homes, destroy careers and ruin lives in a number of different ways. We, more than any other generation in the history of the world, are poisoning ourselves on a massive scale. According to Dr William Pollin, Director of the National Institute on Drug Abuse in the United States of America, more than one quarter of all deaths in America are premature and caused by addiction. Tobacco and alcohol alone kill half a million Americans every year.

In Britain things are much the same. In an official Government publication in December 1984, Professor Griffith Edwards, Director of the Addiction Research Unit at the Institute of Psychiatry in London, was reported to have claimed that in Britain 100,000 people die prematurely each year because of smoking habits, while 700,000 people have a serious alcohol problem. To these figures must be added the fact that many addicts accidentally overdose on illegal drugs or die as a result of injecting themselves with non-sterile needles. The rates of mortality and poor health caused by heroin, glue and other addictive substances are all rising.

As a final irony, drug dependence is the commonest doctor-induced disease. At a conservative estimate, some

250,000 people in Britain have been taking tranquillisers for seven years or more – and are addicted.

The size and significance of the addiction problem is increased by the fact that the majority of addicts, whether they are alcoholics or glue sniffers, heroin users or tranquilliser victims, cause pain, heartache and agony to those around them. Each case of addiction acts like a small explosion, involving and destroying wives, husbands, parents, children, brothers, sisters, friends, neighbours, workmates, employers and just about everyone else with whom the addict comes into contact. There may be one, two or three million people in Britain with an alcohol problem but there are probably five times that many people whose lives are indirectly affected by alcoholism.

Whose life has not been touched by addiction of some sort?

False assumptions about addiction

Although addiction is now a major international problem, the very enormity of the problem has been constantly underestimated for a number of reasons.

Many people still have a very narrow view of what is a 'drug' and what is an 'addict'. Adults who happily drink themselves silly and who chain smoke cigarettes get very upset about children who sniff glue, or smoke or snort heroin. And people who use benzodiazepine tranquillisers become indignant about those using cannabis. Our attitudes and prejudices are, of course, determined by our circumstances, social position, personal experiences, family, and our local laws and customs. In Manhattan, a business executive will think nothing of a three martini lunch. In the Andes, a hill worker will chew coca leaves (from which cocaine is produced). In Jamaica, a labourer will use cannabis to give himself energy.

Patterns of drug use are embedded in our culture and society and there is no readily accepted, legally approved drug in the world that is not now, or has not been in the past, the subject of a vigorous campaign of suppression in another culture or at another time in history.

A number of useless and purely pedantic arguments have confused the picture even more and have contributed to the size of our current problem by encouraging a false sense of security among politicians, doctors and drug users.

For example, there have been attempts to divide drugs into 'hard' and 'soft' categories. Drugs such as heroin and cocaine were classified in the first group, while drugs such as the benzodiazepine tranquillisers were thought to be less troublesome and therefore described as 'soft'. This classification has been shown to be quite without logical scientific foundation, for the benzodiazepine tranquillisers can be as dangerous and as addictive as any of the 'hard' drugs.

There have been attempts to differentiate between 'dependence', 'addiction' and 'habituation'. For many years the amphetamines were regarded as producing nothing more than a mild habituation. It was argued that they could not be considered addictive. This attitude led to widespread over-prescribing of the amphetamine drugs and to much misery and drug-induced unhappiness. Today, most experts accept that any drug which affects the human mind must be addictive, and that the words 'addiction', 'dependence' and 'habituation' are interchangeable.

Some experts argue that there are major differences between physically addictive drugs and psychologically addictive drugs. They say that drugs in the former category have such an effect on the human body that the user will suffer genuine physical symptoms if he stops taking them. The implication has always been that psychological addiction is less fearsome and easier to deal with than physical addiction. Today, the evidence suggests that it is exceedingly difficult to differentiate between the symptoms and signs of physical addiction and those of psychological addiction. The two are far more closely linked than most experts ever imagined. It is now clear that psychological addiction can be just as devastating and destructive as any other addiction.

The other major error made by those studying addiction has been to assume that it is possible to define each drug's addictive qualities in a very specific way. In practice, this has

merely added to the confusion because it is not the pharmacological properties of a drug that make it addictive. It is a
combination of the drug's qualities, the user's individual
personality and his circumstances. For example, alcohol can
have many different effects on different people at different
times. At a party, people will respond in a variety of ways to
similar amounts of alcohol.

The picture has been blurred even further by the fact that
modern scientists have produced a range of refined products
which often have properties that vary enormously from those
of the original drug.

Cocaine is derived from the coca leaf, but the two
substances have very different qualities. Heroin is obtained
from opium, but is considerably more powerful. Deviant
patterns of drug use frequently involve these more modern,
concentrated versions of traditional drugs.

Our attitudes towards addicts and their addictions need
revising thoroughly. In any court of law where an individual
is being tried for a drug offence the chances are high that the
majority of people involved in the legal process will also be
drug addicts of one sort or another. Indeed, it is probable that
most of them will be addicted to drugs (such as tobacco,
alcohol and benzodiazepine tranquillisers) which are *more*
dangerous than the drug which the prisoner is on trial for
possessing. Luck, circumstances and social and environmental factors quite outside individual control determine the
type of product that an individual will choose.

How the problems escalated

Together these factors explain why our drug problem has
reached such an enormous size without being properly recognised. But they don't explain how we acquired such an enormous problem. Again, there are several influencing factors.
The most important of these has undoubtedly been the rate at
which we have changed our world during the last hundred
years, by major developments in communications, transport,
agriculture and so on. These have affected us in many fundamental ways.

treatment programme they release the addict back into exactly the same circumstances and social surroundings as he was in before. Then they are surprised to find that he picks up his old bad habits again. They have done nothing to change the addict's self-image, motivation or lifestyle.

Hope for the future

With addicts squeezed between aggressive, threatening pushers, punitive representatives of the legislative system and the harassed, unimaginative, over-pressured medical profession, it is not surprising that the burden of providing care and comfort, support and succour, has fallen largely on the shoulders of friends and relatives. The damage done by this greatest and most destructive 20th-century plague has not been confined to addicts. Instead, it has involved many millions of innocent and well meaning people, who, fired by a mixture of love, guilt, fear and compassion, have struggled to deal with social, mental, emotional, spiritual and physical demands for which they usually have no training and have not in any way been prepared.

In this book I take a straightforward look at the types of addiction most commonly causing problems in the world today. I analyse the reasons why there are so many drug pushers and the ways in which addicts and addictions are treated. And I point to what I think are solutions to what is undoubtedly the greatest health problem of the 20th century. I hope *Addicts and Addictions* helps the many millions who are addicted, and those whose job it is to provide assistance and care. I also hope, most sincerely, that it helps the countless millions of relatives and friends who have, for too long, carried a burden that our society has failed to share. It is to them that this book is dedicated.

2

ADDICTIONS

Alcohol
Amphetamines
Barbiturates
Benzodiazepines
Cannabis
Cocaine
Diconal (see under Heroin)
Glues and other solvents
Heroin, Morphine and
  Opium
LSD and hallucinogens
Mescaline (see under LSD)

Methadone (see under
  Heroin)
Pethidine (see under Heroin)
Psilocybin (see under LSD)
Tobacco

Other prescription drugs
Non-prescription drugs

Exercise
Food
Gambling
Work

The addictions which have attracted most publicity in recent years are those involving such substances as heroin, cocaine and glue. But although these drugs undoubtedly do cause much misery and unhappiness, they are, in simple statistical terms, relatively minor problems.

The three commonest types of addiction involve alcohol, benzodiazepine drugs and tobacco; there are at least 10 times as many people hooked on any one of the 'Big Three' drugs as there are hooked on all the illegal drugs put together. The amount of anguish, pain and sorrow produced by alcohol and the benzodiazepines far exceeds the amount of anguish, pain and sorrow produced by heroin, cocaine and the other illegal drugs.

In this chapter I have dealt at length with both the common and the uncommon sources of addiction; with the types of addiction only common in our larger cities and with the types of addiction common in every city, town and village. I have even dealt with some non-drug addictions such as food, work and exercise.

In each section I have included advice about how best individual addicts can be helped and I have included specific advice about how to recognise an addict and what symptoms to look out for.

Although there are variations in the way that different addictions may present themselves, there is very little difference in the way that addicts can be helped. I have, therefore, prepared a series of special advice sections describing precisely how best friends and relatives can help addicts most effectively. Since these sections provide general advice (dealing with emergencies, withdrawal and ways to help an addict) they can be found at the back of this book on pages 166, 169 and 165 respectively.

ALCOHOL

■ SIGNS OF ADDICTION

Alcoholics tend to have just one purpose in life – obtaining and using alcohol. Consequently, they lose interest in other aspects of life; they lose time from work, avoid friends, stop caring about relatives, end emotional and sexual relationships and give up long-established hobbies.

Alcoholics tend to be very secretive about what they are doing, where they are going, and why. They lie a good deal. They will steal from their dearest friends and nearest relatives in order to buy alcohol. They make promises they do not keep (and have no intention of keeping). In some extreme cases they may become dirty and unkempt. Money problems may become acute.

Physical symptoms include hand tremor and shakiness, indigestion, poor appetite, impotence, fits, blackouts, memory lapses, and an increased tendency towards accidental injury. They are also likely to suffer from anxiety and depression, lack of concentration, and difficulty in sleeping normally – they may be restless for large parts of the night, experiencing night sweats and terrors.

Alcoholics may also get into trouble with the police for being drunk and disorderly or for drinking and driving. Anyone who has committed more than one such offence needs help.

■ LONG TERM POSSIBLE EFFECTS

Alcohol taken in excess can produce liver damage and brain damage.

■ WITHDRAWAL EFFECTS

The DTs (*delirium tremens*) experienced by alcoholics 'kicking' their habit may include: depression, sleeplessness, sweats, nausea, confusion, anxiety, tremors and vomiting, and sometimes vivid and frightening hallucinations.

■ GIVING UP

If an alcoholic is to break his habit successfully then he must first of all recognise that he has a problem. He must also genuinely want to stop drinking. There is nothing any expert or relative can do which will help an alcoholic who does not want to be helped.

The genuine alcoholic must also accept that if he is going to kick his habit successfully he must give up alcohol completely – for life. The heavy drinker may be able to control his drinking, but the alcoholic must avoid alcohol altogether. Each day must be regarded as a new challenge.

Even the relatively modest amounts of alcohol available in cough medicines and trifles, or sipped at Holy Communion, can prove disastrous.

Medical help should be sought when an alcoholic is suffering from *delirium tremens*, and any physical problems produced by alcohol should be thoroughly investigated and properly treated. It is always worth asking your family doctor for advice and support. He may be able to help by prescribing a sedative (chlormethiazole is probably the most commonly used product, but should only be used for a week or 10 days since it can itself be addictive), and also by prescribing drugs such as disulfiram (often prescribed as Antabuse) which produce a fairly violent feeling of nausea if any alcohol is taken and effectively boost the individual's determination not to drink.

A good family doctor is able to help considerably with counselling and support. The alcoholic's relatives often need just as much help, understanding and encouragement as the alcoholic himself. Most family doctors know of a psychiatrist who can help deal with psychological problems which may have led to the individual's need to drink excessively. If these underlying problems are not dealt with successfully then attempts to give up alcohol are likely to fail.

In some areas behavioural or aversion therapy is available. This helps boost the alcoholic's determination not to drink by teaching him to associate drinking with some immediately unpleasant physical experience, such as an electric shock. However, behavioural therapy is usually only available after referral to a psychiatrist who has a psychologist working with him.

Despite the value of the work done by the experts, the alcoholic and his relatives will gain most support from Alcoholics Anonymous – an excellent organisation which is run by alcoholics for alcoholics (see page 155 and 171 for details). A good family doctor will put the alcoholic determined to avoid drinking in touch with the nearest branch of AA.

See pages 165–172 for general advice on helping an addict, emergencies, giving up and where to find help.

Alcohol is a powerful and potentially destructive substance, and yet its use has been widely accepted throughout Europe and North America for centuries. In countries that have helped to pass powerful, restrictive legislation on substances as innocuous as cannabis, alcohol – an extremely potent drug – is accepted as the one culturally sanctioned intoxicant. Cocaine and opium are banned and their users vilified and persecuted, but alcohol retains a special status as a food, as a sacred drink, and as an aid to celebrations. Although a few attempts have been made to control its production and distribution, countless farmers and businessmen have made legal fortunes out of its sale.

Men have used alcohol for thousands of years. Today it is more easily produced and more widely available than a great many other substances whose effect on mood, perception or behaviour are regarded with fear and suspicion. Indeed, all the evidence suggests that the production and consumption of alcohol is increasing at a tremendous rate. A study of 97 countries showed that between 1960 and 1972 the production of alcoholic beverages rose by over 60 percent. In developing countries and even in those countries where alcohol is illegal, its consumption is rising rapidly. These days countries are losing their individual drinking patterns; everyone, women and teenagers included, is using alcohol.

As long ago as 1974, the World Health Organization's Expert Committee on Drug Dependence concluded that, 'in many parts of the world problems associated with the use of alcohol far exceed those associated with the non-medical use of less socially accepted dependence producing drugs such as those of the amphetamine and morphine types.'

Reasons for increased consumption

The sale of alcohol has become a major international industry. In Britain, where the consumption of alcohol has doubled in the last 30 years, the production, marketing and selling of alcoholic drinks employs over three quarters of a million people. Alcohol exports earn the country over £1,000 million a year, and in 1983 alone the tax raised on alcohol exceeded £5,000 million. In some countries the figures are even more astonishing. In France, for example, something like ten percent of the entire workforce earn their living in the production or sale of alcohol. All round the world the taxes raised by the production and sale of alcoholic drinks make up a substantial part of Government revenue. In developing countries the establishment of a brewing industry is often one of the first steps towards industrialisation.

The industry's influence on our drinking habits are numerous and varied. It is in the brewing industry's best interests to keep alcohol prices as low as possible, so they lobby politicians to ensure that taxes don't get out of hand. The industry also spends huge amounts of money in trying to persuade us to buy its products. Once again, the industry's hold over the Government means that there are very few restrictions on advertising. Much of it is sophisticated and extremely effective. The copywriters use sex and status to sell us their products and they have succeeded in making alcohol one of the standard Christmas gifts.

The fact that alcohol is obtainable legally means that people who wouldn't dream of using any dubious or 'illegal' prop are happy to use it as an aid in dealing with stress and pressure. Indeed, alcohol isn't just a legally obtainable drug, it is the one psychoactive substance that is regularly sanitised by the political and ecclesiastical establishments. Catholics, Protestants and Jews celebrate religious festivals with alcohol. Socially, just about every dinner or toast, speech or public function is celebrated with alcohol. We even launch a new boat by smashing a bottle of champagne over its bow. This social acceptability means that alcohol is usually the first substance most law-abiding citizens reach for when things start getting tough.

The wide availability of alcohol has also had a powerful effect on its popularity. All the evidence suggests that when alcohol is sold in self-service stores and supermarkets there is a local increase in the amount of alcohol being drunk. The availability of home brewing kits has had a similar effect on consumption. The easier it is to get hold of alcohol, the more people there will be drinking too much of it. Allowing super-market chains to sell wine, beer and spirits alongside breakfast cereals and fresh fruit has undoubtedly had an important effect on the number of people drinking to excess.

Women alcoholics

The fact that alcohol is now readily available in corner shops and supermarkets probably helps to explain why there are so many women alcoholics. It's effective. It's acceptable. And you can pick it up and take it home with the cat food and the washing powder. No one will notice or think anything of it. Ten years ago there were eight men to every one woman with a real drinking problem. Today, there are only three times as many men with a drinking problem. Among women aged between 30 and 50, alcoholism has become rife. On a nice, neat, modern housing estate, where there are countless women locked into loneliness and embittered by boredom, there will be alcoholics behind a staggering number of neatly painted doors. The ones who aren't hooked on alcohol are likely to be hooked on tranquillisers. And many are hooked on both.

They start drinking because of boredom, anxiety, frus-tration and loneliness. To begin with, it is easy. There is no difficulty in getting supplies, and there may even be some social cachet in being able to drink the men under the table. By the time the habit has become an addiction and it is too late to stop, the woman drinker will be consumed with guilt and shame. Once those destructive emotions are added to her original loneliness, boredom and frustration, her drinking problem will be complete.

The physical problems

Many people still believe that the only organ likely to be damaged by drinking is the liver. Sadly, that is not true.

People who drink heavily risk developing cancer, stomach ulcers and muscle wastage as well as liver disease.

Women who drink too much and get pregnant run a real risk of having backward or low birth-weight babies. They also run an increased risk of developing physical problems such as liver disease, for the female body is physiologically more vulnerable than the male body to the adverse effects of alcohol.

Apart from these physical effects, however, it is the effects it has on the brain that makes alcohol particularly dangerous. Alcohol is detectable in the brain within half a minute of a glass being emptied.

Basically, alcohol is a depressant. If you drink a modest amount the depressant effect seems to work most noticeably on the part of the brain that controls your tendency to get excited. With the controls depressed you become more excited and talkative.

Natural social and personal inhibitions are lifted by alcohol and most people, when they have had a drink or two, become much looser and less restricted. A quiet individual may become very talkative, and a shy person may become aggressive. Under the influence of alcohol, a fellow who is normally very cautious may stop worrying about what people think. At the same time, the brain's ability to concentrate on information, understand messages it is receiving and make judgements on those messages will diminish. Reflexes will go, and although the individual won't be aware of it, his ability to link sensory input to muscular function will be badly distorted. So, the person who has been drinking will think that he or she will be able to talk, dance or drive a car more efficiently than normal, whereas, in fact, his ability to do any of these things will be adversely affected.

Eventually, the depressant effect of alcohol affects other areas of brain function, and finally the individual will appear drunken and will probably fall into a stupor.

The results of all this damage are difficult to overestimate. A few bald statistics from around the world will probably illustrate the point. In France, which has the highest consumption of alcohol per head, and where 80 percent of the people think that wine is good for health and 25 percent think it is quite indispensable, 10 percent of all deaths are directly due to the excessive consumption of alcohol. In Britain, 20 percent of male admissions to general medical wards are related to the use of alcohol. In 1980, approximately half a million admissions to general medical wards were caused by excessive drinking. In countries as varied as America, Australia and Argentina, between one third and one half of all the people admitted to psychiatric hospitals need psychiatric in-patient help because of their excessive drinking habits.

The risks of alcoholism

A major risk for a drinker is that he will become an alcoholic – a drinker trapped by his need to keep drinking. According to World Health Organization figures, between 1 percent and 10 percent of the world's population is dependent on alcohol and disabled by drinking. Anyone who cannot control when he starts drinking and when he stops drinking is an alcoholic – however much alcohol is involved.

Experts argue about just how much a drinker needs to consume to become an alcoholic, but the consensus of opinion seems to be that if you drink five pints of beer or a third of a pint of whisky a day, then you are in trouble. Something like one in every three drinkers is already in this category or is heading for it.

The risks involved in being an alcoholic are devastating. An alcoholic is about four times as likely to die in any given year as a non-drinker of the same age, sex and economic status. Alcoholics are more likely to be involved in accidents and to develop serious liver disease or cancer.

Stages to becoming an alcoholic

Most people who become addicted to alcohol start by drinking socially but quickly learn that alcohol provides some relief from stress and pressure and day to day psychological problems. As a result, the drinker starts turning more and more to the bottle.

The rate at which things get out of control depends upon a number of factors: the age and sex of the individual, his or her family history (there is a hereditary factor involved and if both your parents were alcoholics then you have an increased risk of becoming an alcoholic yourself), and the pressure the individual is under. But however long it takes to get there, the next stage is usually pretty much the same for most budding alcoholics.

He will start drinking secretly, feeling guilty about his drinking, and drinking in the mornings as well as the evenings. He will also need to increase his intake of alcohol in order to survive comfortably. He may well keep on drinking until he gets physically sick. At this stage he has a tremendous tolerance for drink.

The alcoholic's home and work life begin to suffer. His failures at home and at work will make him feel aggressive and resentful. When he loses friends, gets thrown out of home or is fired from work he'll feel aggrieved and drink more in order to try to cope. It is at this point that he may become violent, physically attacking his wife or children. Wife battering and baby battering are a common side effect of alcoholism.

He's likely to smell of alcohol at odd times of the day, although he may try to disguise this by using a powerful aftershave. (Women alcoholics have an advantage here for they can douse themselves in perfume. However the quantity and quality of the perfume will usually give them away.) He will probably have a regular hand tremor that makes it difficult for him to write legibly and he may develop chronic indigestion. He will worry if he hasn't got supplies at hand and will keep a bottle of his favourite beverage in an office drawer or kitchen cupboard, drinking alone and in secret for most of the time. He will lie about his drinking habits, and probably have the occasional blackout. He will steal if necessary in order to buy supplies, and probably drink just about anything he can lay his hands on.

In the final stages of alcoholism he will drink for days at a time, get completely drunk and stay that way. He will take no care of his physical appearance and won't bother too much about food. He will get frightened and suffer tremors. He may even become less tolerant to alcohol and, as his liver functions less and less well, need less in order to get drunk.

This situation is by no means uncommon. Alcoholism and tranquilliser addiction are the commonest types of drug addiction. There are said to be between nine and 10 million alcoholics in the United States of America alone. There may be up to three million alcoholics in Britain. There are many millions more around the world.

Effects of withdrawal

As soon as the alcoholic tries to manage without a drink he will start to suffer from the 'alcohol withdrawal syndrome'. Within six to eight hours of stopping drinking he'll start to sweat and feel sick, and his limbs will tremble. Later he will be confused, disorientated, restless, frightened and paranoid. He will have hallucinations (imagining that he can see rats, spiders, toads, snakes or demons, or that he is surrounded by policemen) and begin shaking. He may start having fits and may become violent. He will be suffering from what is commonly known as *delirium tremens*. Since this condition may last for several days, during which time the alcoholic will need constant supervision, patients should be admitted to a hospital or specialist clinic for 'drying out'.

Why alcohol?

Just why people reach this terrible stage is difficult to explain. There is some evidence to show that some people are 'born' to become alcoholics and will eventually end up drinking too much whatever else happens to them. And it is certainly true that because we live in a social climate that accepts and generally approves of drinking as a way of relieving tension and emotional problems, it is remarkably easy for anyone who feels insecure or who lacks affection to turn to alcohol for support.

But there are purely physical factors involved too. Take any of the addictive drugs to excess and you will get hooked and eventually stop functioning effectively *without* that drug. Alcohol is an addictive drug and anyone taking an excess will become addicted. The real problem is that the amount involved can vary enormously from individual to individual and we still don't have any way of determining which individuals are most likely to develop alcoholism or how much alcohol they can safely consume.

Social effects of alcohol

Another major problem associated with alcohol is that, apart from being a very destructive drug in personal terms, it is also immensely harmful in social terms. In 1979, the 32nd World Health Assembly declared that 'problems related to alcohol, and particularly to its excessive consumption, rank among the world's major public health problems' and 'constitute serious hazards for human health, welfare and life.'

Alcohol is said to cause between a third and a half of all road deaths in developed countries. It causes about a third of all accidents at work. It adversely affects the abilities of politicians and businessmen, of doctors and entertainers. It is involved in a third of all divorces and a third of all child abuse cases. Between eight and 15 million days of work are lost every year through alcohol.

In America it has been confirmed that more than 75 percent of police time is spent on alcohol related crimes, that the vast majority of criminals are heavy drinkers and that about one half of all murders are alcohol-related, in that either the victim or the murderer had been drinking.

In Britain, research reported in the *British Journal of Addiction* in 1983 showed that 64 percent of all people arrested had been drinking in the four hours prior to their arrest, while among people arrested between 10 p.m. and 2 a.m. 93 percent had been drinking heavily. Even among the under-18 year-olds arrested, 65 percent had been drinking. Alcohol is a significant factor in about 1,000 arrests every day in Britain.

In the past, attempts to control the use of alcohol were based largely on moral grounds. It was repeatedly pointed out that alcohol has a destructive effect on personal morality, on family life, on an individual's ability and willingness to work and on behaviour in the streets.

Those arguments have now been overshadowed and superseded by more urgent and demanding ones.

Alcohol is no longer a subject of concern to individual, isolated families. The problems have become so immense that they should worry us all: alcoholics and non-alcoholics, drinkers and non-drinkers alike.

For general advice on emergencies, giving up and where to find help, see pages 165–172.

AMPHETAMINES

■ SIGNS OF ADDICTION

Amphetamine users tend to be very thin because their appetites are poor; edgy, unable to keep still and unable to sleep. Most amphetamine users take their drugs by mouth but some use the drug intravenously, in which case there may be tell-tale needle marks – usually where the veins can easily be reached. The most popular sites are the forearms, particularly in the bend at the inside of the elbow. When these veins get worn out by over-use, addicts will use any vein that they can find. Some try to avoid using the veins in the arms since they know that these are the ones most commonly examined. Addicts who do not use clean equipment or techniques frequently have infected sores at injection sites.

Amphetamine users tend to have just one purpose in life – obtaining and using amphetamine. As a result, they may lose interest in their family, work and friends. They may become unusually secretive and exceptionally dishonest. If they have to buy their amphetamines, they may start stealing (even from close friends and relatives). They will make promises that they cannot keep. Amphetamine addicts may also get into trouble with the police –

commonly for stealing prescription pads and forging signatures.

■ LONG TERM POSSIBLE EFFECTS

Amphetamine taken for long periods can produce liver damage, severe mental problems, delusions and hallucinations.

■ WITHDRAWAL EFFECTS

When amphetamine is withdrawn from a long-term user, the effects usually include sleepiness, tiredness, irritability and depression.

■ GIVING UP

If the amphetamine was obtained legally from a doctor (for example as a slimming aid), then I suggest changing doctors. Most doctors disapprove of the overprescribing of amphetamines and will be happy to help addicts cut down their dosage gradually. In order to minimise the mental depression and feeling of tiredness which usually accompanies the withdrawal of amphetamines, I suggest that amphetamines be cut down at the same rate as benzodiazepines (see page 31).

If the amphetamine was obtained illegally, then I suggest that the user ask his (or her) own doctor for help. An honest confession should elicit a sympathetic response.

As with other types of addiction, it is important to find out why the addiction began. If circumstances and pressures are not altered, the addict is likely to begin using amphetamine again soon after giving up.

For general advice on helping an addict, emergencies, giving up and where to find help, see pages 165–172.

Amphetamines were first synthesised in Los Angeles in 1927, but were not introduced on a large scale until the 1930s.

Quite early on, however, it was recognised that the drug was addictive. When the psychological effects of amphetamine were first being investigated, students took supplies and used it as an unofficial (and presumably illegal) stimulant. In 1933, researchers Oswald and Thacore pointed out that amphetamine continues to have an effect upon the brain long after the drug has been withdrawn. By 1938 it was known that addiction was a real risk.

This hazard wasn't taken too seriously by the authorities for amphetamine was found to be useful as a stimulant and a source of energy. During the Spanish Civil War amphetamines were included in survival packs, and during the Second World War both sides used the drugs. Something like 72 million amphetamine tablets were issued to British troops to help them keep fighting for prolonged periods; German paratroopers were also given additional energy this way. In Japan, the amphetamines were not just used to help keep soldiers fighting for long periods; they were also used to increase efficiency in factories.

After the Second World War (by which time many people had discovered that amphetamines reduced the appetite and were therefore useful for anyone who wanted to diet), it was officially recognised by some experts that the amphetamines did cause problems. People who used the drug became depressed and miserable as the effect wore off, needing to take more amphetamine pills in order to control their depression.

All around the world attempts were made to control what was clearly becoming a major addiction problem. Attempts to deal with the drug were most successful in Japan, where amphetamine control laws were brought in and in 1951 over 17,000 people were arrested. When the number of people taking amphetamines didn't fall, the Japanese introduced a major campaign against the drug and the results were impressive. In 1955, when the campaign was launched, 29 people in Japan were arrested for murder stemming from the use of amphetamines. By 1957 this figure had fallen to zero and the number of arrests for amphetamine misuse had also fallen dramatically.

The Japanese were, however, something of an exception. In other countries attempts to control the amphetamines were far less successful. In Britain, the campaign against them was very weak and unenthusiastic. In 1954, the Chief Medical Officer at the Ministry of Health described amphetamines as non toxic, without serious side effects and non-addictive. In 1959, 2.5 percent of all National Health Service prescriptions were for preparations containing an amphetamine or similar products. The total number of prescriptions for that year was 5,600,000.

One reason why the amphetamines remained uncontrolled for so long in Britain, and in some other countries, was undoubtedly the fact that a major debate was going on between those doctors who believed that amphetamines caused addiction and those who argued that they caused habituation. The World Health Organization's Expert Committee on Addiction-Producing Drugs repeatedly emphasised that a distinction between addiction and habituation was both useful and valid. Physicians and companies who wanted to keep the amphetamines in circulation took full advantage of this, claiming that the amphetamines caused habituation (a psychological need) rather than addiction (a physical or physiological need) – the former being regarded as a much less worrying problem. In *The Amphetamines, their actions and uses* by Leake, published in 1958, the pedantic argument about addiction and dependence was discussed. 'Both clinical and experimental studies,' wrote the author, 'agree in acknowledging that habituation to the use of amphetamine may occur, but that addiction, in the sense defined by the World Health Organization, is extremely rare and not satisfactorily substantiated.'

In Britain, the problem continued to get bigger through the late 1950s and the 1960s. By 1966 general practitioners working in the National Health Service were prescribing 200 million amphetamine tablets a year, and many middle-aged women had taken to forgery in order to keep getting supplies of their drug.

The pattern was bad enough in Britain, but in America it

had reached colossal proportions. In 1966, the Food and Drug Administration in the United States estimated that over 25 tons of amphetamines (half the annual domestic production) found its way into illegal channels – enough to provide everyone in America with 14 tablets a year. It was estimated that year that in Oklahoma City (which had a population of 300,000) there were 5,000 addicts.

While drug companies continued to promote the amphetamines for a wide range of symptoms (as late as 1974 Smith Kline and French were selling amphetamines for the treatment of 'mild and temporary emotional distress', 'mild transient depressive states', 'appetite suppression in obesity', 'nocturnal enuresis and certain 'hyperkinetic states and behaviour disorders in children', and for 'pain relief') and large numbers of people were getting hooked on amphetamines prescribed for them, millions more were discovering the amphetamines through the black market. By the mid 1960s, teenage 'Mods' were regularly using amphetamines, which they usually knew as 'purple hearts'. They used the drug to help them keep going through all-night parties and to help suppress the tedium and boredom of ordinary working life. In the 1960s the use of intravenous amphetamine had an unexpected boost when laws were introduced to try to control the growing epidemic of heroin abuse.

Throughout the 1970s the problem of amphetamine addiction continued to worry many authorities. Yet drug companies carried on manufacturing amphetamines and promoting them as slimming aids. In America, the opposition to prescribing amphetamines was powerful and effective. In New York a Bill was passed making it illegal for doctors to prescribe amphetamines for slimmers. The State Medical Society which, like other such organisations, usually opposes attempts to limit doctors' freedom, did not oppose this particular legislation. Similar legislation passed in Wisconsin had a dramatic effect, with the sale of amphetamines falling to almost zero. In Britain the story was quite different: two drugs, Durophet and Dexedrine, both of which contained amphetamine drug types, were still available well into the 1980s, and a number of doctors made a very comfortable living from writing out private prescriptions for these two products.

Today, amphetamines are no longer recommended for the treatment of overweight patients. (The one condition for which the amphetamines *are* still recommended is narcolepsy, a disorder in which the patient keeps falling asleep unexpectedly and needs to take regular stimulants in order to stay awake. Inevitably, addicts have learned to fake the symptoms of narcolepsy in order to persuade doctors to prescribe amphetamines for them.) But the drug companies haven't quite finished working the rich amphetamine seam. Drugs which stimulate the central nervous system are still available. And the British Government has once again been slow in bringing in controlling legislation.

Even now, there are hundreds of thousands of amphetamine addicts. But since only about four million amphetamine tablets are prescribed legally each year, many undoubtedly obtain their supplies illegally. Amphetamine production is fairly easy and cheap to organise, and the drug companies, the Government and the medical profession have produced a huge reservoir of customers for the black market suppliers to exploit.

See also pages 165–172 for general advice on emergencies, giving up and where to find help.

BARBITURATES

■ SIGNS OF ADDICTION
Barbiturate users invariably suffer from tremors, irritability, fits, sleeplessness and agitation. They may have blackouts, find it difficult to concentrate, and have more accidents than usual. They tend to be unusually secretive.

If they obtain their barbiturate supplies illegally, they may have money problems and may start stealing, even from those who are close to them. The side effects associated with barbiturates are, in general, similar to the effects associated with alcohol.

■ LONG TERM POSSIBLE EFFECTS

Barbiturate users may develop fits and mental problems such as depression. When taken in overdose, barbiturates are often lethal. Even a small accidental overdose can kill.

■ WITHDRAWAL EFFECTS

Users coming off barbiturates may have difficulty in sleeping and may have nightmares. They are also likely to become very anxious and irritable and suffer tremors. They may have fits. In general the withdrawal effects of barbiturates are very similar to those associated with alcohol (see page 10). When long-acting barbiturates have been used the withdrawal effects may not develop for several days.

■ GIVING UP

If the barbiturates were obtained legally from a doctor (for example, as a sleeping aid), then I suggest changing doctors. Most doctors disapprove of the overprescribing of barbiturates and will be happy to help addicts cut down their dosage gradually.

If the barbiturates were obtained illegally, then I suggest that the user ask his or her own doctor for help. An honest confession should elicit a sympathetic response.

Because of the risk of fits, barbiturates should be given up under close medical supervision. It is important that the drugs should not be stopped suddenly but should be reduced gradually over a period of time. The length of time needed for withdrawal depends on the size of the dose that has been taken, the length of time for which it was used, and the type of barbiturate.

As with other types of addiction, it is important to find out why it began. If circumstances and pressures are not altered, the addict is likely to begin taking barbiturates again soon after giving up.

For general advice on helping an addict, emergencies, giving up and finding help, see pages 165–172.

Barbituric acid was first prepared in 1864 by 29-year-old Adolph von Baeyer, who was working as a research chemist in Ghent. There are several different stories describing how the drug got its name, but in the one I like best Baeyer is said to have gone out to celebrate his discovery in a nearby pub – and found himself drinking alongside a group of local officers celebrating St Barbara's Day. It's probably apocryphal but it's a pleasant story.

Since then more than 25,000 different barbiturates have been produced, and about 50 of them marketed for use. They are usually prescribed to help nervous, troubled, anxious people, or as sleeping pills for sufferers from insomnia. There has never been any doubt that the barbiturates are effective sedatives.

First signs of problems

The problems associated with their use first became apparent in the early 1950s when one writer pointed out that the addiction of patients to barbiturates was more serious than the addiction of patients to morphine. At the United States Public Health Services Addiction Research Centre in Lexington, Kentucky, research workers did some important work with five volunteers which showed that after taking the drugs for a mere three months, withdrawal produced psychoses, epileptic convulsions and other serious symptoms.

By 1970 it was clear that hundreds of thousands of people were addicted to the barbiturates. Dr F. O. Wells of Ipswich, writing in the journal of the Royal College of General Practitioners in 1973, described how he and his partners had decided to give up prescribing barbiturates for anything other than the treatment of convulsions because of the high risk of suicide among patients taking the drug. In America the barbiturates were said to be killing 10,000 people a year, while in 1972 in Britain the barbiturates were said to be responsible for 1,000 suicide deaths. A psychiatrist in America developed a successful way of treating patients over the age of 50 who were forgetful and confused – he simply took them off their barbiturates. And a growing number of researchers around the world were confirming the Lexington experiment and proving that the barbiturates *were* addictive and potentially dangerous drugs.

In 1975 there were said to be 500,000 regular barbiturate users in the United Kingdom, of whom something like 100,000 were hooked. It was acknowledged that the barbiturates – thought at one time to have a temporary effect rather like alcohol – caused personality deterioration and terrible bouts of anxiety. Even so, thousands of general practitioners still prescribed them for patients who couldn't get to sleep or who wanted something to calm their nerves a little. In the mid 1970s the barbiturates were *still* the most commonly prescribed drugs for the treatment of anxiety and insomnia.

Curbing the problems

In the late 1970s a fairly successful anti-barbiturate campaign was run in Britain. Organised by a small number of determined doctors, the Campaign for the Use and Restriction of Barbiturates (known inevitably as CURB) helped to spread the word among members of the medical profession and by 1978 the number of prescriptions being written for barbiturates in Britain was down to 5,000,000 a year. Some addicts, deprived of their pills, turned to the black market and the decline in the availability of barbiturates was matched by an increase in the availability of illegally imported heroin. Other addicts stayed with their family doctors but changed from the barbiturates (out of fashion with the medical profession) to the benzodiazepines (very much in fashion among doctors).

The number of doctors prescribing barbiturates continued to fall through the early 1980s. By 1984 the number of barbiturate prescriptions written for patients who had never previously taken the drug was down to 76,000. There were, however, still many thousands of addicted barbiturate users getting regular repeat prescriptions from family doctors. In January 1985, when the size of the problem had been dramatically reduced in Britain, the Government finally brought many of the common barbiturates under the prescribing requirements of the *Misuse of Drugs Act* 1973.

The new legislation was greeted with enthusiasm by the benzodiazepine manufacturers, and a few days after the regulations came into force one of the country's medical magazines carried a full page drug company advertisement which reminded practitioners of the change. The advertisement pointed out that the new regulations would 'result in an extra demand upon the general practitioner's time' and reminded doctors that 'prescriptions [for barbiturates] must be written out by the prescriber in full and in ink'. The copywriter then went on to name one of the benzodiazepine drugs which 'has established itself as an effective hypnotic with ten years of clinical experience behind it' and to boast that three studies had been conducted specifically to assess the value of the drug in barbiturate substitution. The three studies referred to included two dating back to 1975 and 1976, both of which were published in the *Journal of International Medical Research*, which, as I pointed out in my book *Paper Doctors* in 1977, is slightly unusual in that it charges drug companies to print material on its 'editorial' pages. The price per page in 1975 was £85 – a cheap price to pay for the right to quote an apparently sound scientific reference.

In Britain the barbiturates have undoubtedly had their day. A relatively small number of elderly medical practitioners continue to prescribe them for anxious or sleepless patients. Addiction to the barbiturates, such a massive problem in the 1960s and 1970s, has now largely been replaced by addiction to the benzodiazepines, but it does remain a problem in many countries.

See pages 165–172 for general advice on helping an addict, emergencies, giving up and where to find help.

BENZODIAZEPINES

■ SIGNS OF ADDICTION

Benzodiazepine addicts tend to be depressed, anxious, tired, lethargic and rather unsteady. They may also be secretive about what they are doing. They tend to feel uncomfortable and frightened if their supplies are running low and, like individuals addicted to other substances, may keep supplies hidden around the house. They will often have difficulty in getting to sleep – despite taking sleeping tablets. If they have been obtaining their drugs illegally, then they may have money problems and may start stealing from those close to them.

■ LONG TERM POSSIBLE EFFECTS

Brain damage is possible (although there is some controversy about this).

■ WITHDRAWAL EFFECTS

Addicts giving up benzodiazepines tend to suffer from a variety of symptoms including: tremor and shaking, intense anxiety, dizziness, sleepiness, an inability to concentrate, nausea, a metallic taste in the mouth, depression, headaches. Other effects are clumsiness, an increased sensitivity to light and noise, tiredness, blurred vision, hot and cold feelings, aching muscles, an inability to speak normally, hallucinations, confusion, sweating and fits.

■ GIVING UP

The benzodiazepine user who wants to give up should contact his or her doctor and should always cut down very slowly. The drugs are so easily available that few users will have obtained their supplies illegally. Most will have obtained them from their own family doctor. There is little point in changing doctors unless the doctor who originally prescribed the drug refuses to accept that it can be addictive or potentially dangerous.

The rate at which benzodiazepines are reduced will depend upon the size of the dosage. As a rule of thumb, the dose should be halved every two weeks until it can no longer be halved. So, if six tablets are taken every day, that amount should be reduced to five tablets a day for four days, then to four tablets a day for another four days, then to three tablets a day for four days. In that way the initial dose will be halved in about two weeks. Doctors can help by prescribing lower dose pills to assist with the cutting down procedure. When down to one pill a day it may help to miss alternate day's doses.

I also suggest getting in touch with one of the many voluntary, specialist organisations dealing with tranquilliser addiction (see page 172).

As with other types of addiction, it is important to find out why the addiction began. If circumstances and pressures are not altered the addict may find herself using benzodiazepines again soon after giving up.

See pages 165–172 for general advice on helping an addict, emergencies, giving up and where to find help.

In 1954, while working in America at the New Jersey Laboratories of Hoffman La Roche, Dr Leo H Sternbach started experimenting with two sets of chemicals called benzophenones and heptoxdiazines. Inspired by the success of certain tranquillisers, he hoped that these chemicals might prove to have some useful pharmacological action on the brain.

After producing and investigating some 40 new products, Sternbach still hadn't managed to find anything of commercial value. Indeed, he was so disappointed by the results of his experiments that he put the final drug of the series on a shelf while he turned to other research projects.

Eighteen months later, a laboratory spring clean resulted in this final product, code number Ro5–0690, being sent off to Roche's Director of Pharmacological Research for proper testing. Two months later, in July 1957, the substance was described as being a hypnotic, a relaxant and a sedative. And by the spring of the following year it had been identified as a benzodiazepine – an entirely new substance.

'Over-night' success

From that point on things moved fast: it was discovered that the new benzodiazepine had powerful effects as a relaxant, an anti-convulsant and a treatment for anxiety. By March 1960, the preliminary tests had all been done; the American Food and Drug Administration had approved the drug and it was on the market. It was known as Librium.

That first benzodiazepine was immensely successful. Within months, Roche and other companies were seeking variations on what looked like being an extremely promising theme. The new drug had been shown to relieve anxiety, help people to get to sleep and relax tense and tight muscles. New benzodiazepines followed quickly, with Valium coming on to the market in 1963. The benzodiazepine explosion was tremendous – by 1979 there were said to be about 700 Valium-like substances available.

These new tranquillisers were greeted with enthusiasm by doctors in hospitals and general practice. It seemed that the drugs were both effective and safe, and doctors who were worried about the dangers associated with the barbiturates were delighted to prescribe these new products instead.

In the late 1960s the number of prescriptions for drugs in this group rose steadily, and by 1970 the benzodiazepines and other similar drugs made up approximately 6.5 percent of all drugs prescribed by British general practitioners. By 1975, when the barbiturates were the object of a campaign to reduce prescribing, the total number of prescriptions for tranquillisers was still rising – one out of every six prescriptions was for a drug in this general group.

But still the limits had not been reached. In 1977 a total of 45 million prescriptions for tranquillisers were written, and almost one fifth of all prescriptions were for drugs like Valium and Librium. The benzodiazepines had become the world's most popular drugs.

Reasons for popularity

There were three basic reasons why the benzodiazepines proved so popular.

First, most doctors in practice have grown up in a world where they are accustomed to getting their prescribing information from drug companies. If a drug company tells a doctor that a drug does a particular job and is safe, then the doctor will usually accept that information uncritically.

Second, by the time the benzodiazepines arrived doctors were finding it more and more difficult to hide from the fact that the barbiturates were dangerous. By the mid 1970s there was plenty of evidence to show that the barbiturates were causing an enormous addiction problem. There was a desperate need for an alternative product. And the benzodiazepines fitted the bill perfectly.

Third, doctors desperately needed the benzodiazepines. During the 1950s and 1960s the type of problem being discussed in the doctor's surgery was changing and general practitioners found that they were expected to deal with mental and psychological problems as well as the physical ones. They were consulted by patients who were anxious, depressed, irritable, upset and often just miserable. Through TV programmes and magazine articles, newspaper reports and popular books, millions of men and women were encouraged to regard mental problems as something that could be treated, and persuaded that they need never endure anything remotely resembling unhappiness. The relationship between stress and disease became common knowledge.

Doctors had never been trained to cope with stress-induced problems. Most knew little more about anxiety, depression and psychosomatic disease than their patients. Most doctors practising in the 1960s and 1970s had spent as much time at medical school studying tropical diseases as they had studying psychiatry. The benzodiazepines were an instant solution that doctors welcomed with open arms. Within a short time doctors in every developed country were regularly prescribing these new tranquillisers.

Dangers of addiction

Amid all the enthusiasm for the new drugs a number of muted warnings were sounded. In 1961, just a short time after chlordiazepoxide (the chemical name for Librium) was introduced into clinical practice, a report appeared in *Psychopharmacologia* which was written by three physicians from the Veterans' Administration Hospital, Palo Alta, California. Entitled 'Withdrawal reactions from Chlordiazepoxide ("Librium")', the paper described very dramatically how patients who had been taking the drug suffered from withdrawal symptoms when the drug was stopped. Nor was that an isolated report.

Fourteen years later, in 1975, three doctors from the Drug Dependence Treatment Center at the Philadelphia VA Hospital and University of Pennsylvania, Philadelphia, published a paper in *The International Journal of the Addictions* entitled 'Misuse and Abuse of Diazepam: An Increasingly Common Medical Problem'. Doctors Woody, O'Brien and Greenstein referred to papers published as far back as 1970 which had documented instances of physical addiction to chlordiazepoxide and diazepam. They reported that since the end of 1972 they had noticed an increasing amount of diazepam misuse and abuse. Their paper concluded: 'All physicians should know that diazepam abuse and misuse is occurring and careful attention should be given to prescribing, transporting and storing this drug.'

Similar evidence was appearing in England. In a symposium at the Royal Society of Medicine in April 1973, Dr John Bonn, then a senior lecturer and Consultant Psychiatrist at St Bartholomew's and Hackney Hospitals, London, said that 'The benzodiazepines are medication to be avoided, unless the patient is under close supervision.' He explained that he saw a number of benzodiazepine-dependent patients and that when these patients were weaned off their drugs they often felt much better than they had for years.

By 1979 the evidence had become even more powerful and a psychiatrist testifying to a US Senate health sub committee claimed that patients could become hooked on diazepam in as little as six weeks. The same committee also heard testimony that it is harder to kick the tranquilliser habit than it is to get off heroin. One expert witness said that tranquillisers provided America's number one drug problem, apart from alcohol.

Effects of benzodiazepine

Back in 1968, a report published in the *Journal of the American Medical Association* dealt with eight patients who were taking diazepam in a normal daily dosage of 5 mg three or four times a day. The authors reported that seven patients had such deep depressions while on the drugs that they developed suicidal thoughts and impulses. Two of the patients killed themselves, another two made serious attempts to commit suicide. Five of the patients showed improvements in three or four days after their diazepam had been reduced and stopped.

A report published in 1972, in the *American Journal of Psychiatry*, described how six patients on diazepam had exhibited symptoms which included tremulousness, apprehension, depression and insomnia. Previously, the patients had all been emotionally stable and the symptoms, which all started quite suddenly, were severe. When the patients were taken off diazepam their symptoms disappeared.

In Holland, in 1979, a psychiatrist contributed a paper to a Dutch medical journal in which he described how four patients taking benzodiazepine sleeping tablets had developed severe anxiety and intolerable psychological changes. This report led to about 600 other similar complaints about the drug.

At a conference at the National Institute of Health in Washington, USA, in 1982, a British professor of psychopharmacology reported that brain scans carried out on a small group of patients who had been taking diazepam for a number of years had produced evidence of brain damage. And research reported at a neuro-psychopharmacology conference in Jerusalem in 1982 suggested that the benzodiazepines may affect the human memory. In addition to all this evidence, medical journals around the world carried studies and reports which showed that people who take benzodiazepines and then drive are particularly likely to be involved in road accidents. It was also evident that the benzodiazepines can have an adverse effect on a patient's sex life; that they cause aggression and can produce troublesome interactions when taken at the same time as tea and coffee. They may also have an adverse effect on the developing foetus when taken by a pregnant woman, are too dangerous to be taken by breast-feeding mothers and may cause liver damage. Indeed, in the period from January 1964 to February 1982 the Committee on Safety of Medicines in London received reports about well over 100 different side effects said to be related to the use of diazepam alone. Other benzodiazepines produced their own fearfully impressive list of side effects.

But the major problem with the benzodiazepines remains that they are dangerously addictive. The other side effects and dangers worry many doctors, but the big task for the late 1980s is going to be helping the millions of regular benzodiazepine users to kick their habits. Stopping the benzodiazepines too quickly can produce uncomfortable and sometimes dangerous side effects (see page 30) and most experts recommend that any patient wishing to cut down his or her dosage should only do so under a doctor's supervision. The medical profession has created a new challenge for itself – the world's biggest drug addiction problem.

CANNABIS

■ SIGNS OF ADDICTION

There is a characteristic smell when cannabis is smoked. Sensations such as touch, sound and smell all tend to be heightened and users may experience hallucinations. They may also seem particularly happy and relaxed. Cannabis can be expensive and so regular users may have money problems – although it is relatively rare for cannabis users who do not also use other drugs to run into severe financial difficulties.

Cannabis users frequently get into trouble with the police. They may be arrested for possession of drugs, for dealing in drugs, for growing the drug and so on.

■ LONG TERM POSSIBLE EFFECTS

Occasionally users develop chest problems but physical and mental problems seem to be relatively rare. The main hazard associated with cannabis is that users come into contact with drug pushers selling other, more dangerous products. There are millions of cannabis users and most do not progress to heroin or cocaine. But most heroin or cocaine users started with cannabis.

■ WITHDRAWAL EFFECTS

Heavy users may develop depression, sleeplessness and anxiety when they stop the drug. Tremors are also common.

■ GIVING UP

Cannabis users who want to give up should try cutting down slowly. Cannabis is not particularly addictive and there should not be too many problems during the withdrawal period.

As with other types of addiction it is important to find out why the addiction began. If circumstances and pressures are not altered the addict is likely to begin using cannabis again soon after giving up.

See also pages 165–172 for general advice on helping an addict, emergencies, giving up and where to find help.

Cannabis (also known as Bang, Bhang, Charas, Ganja, Gouge, Grass, Hash, Hasheesh, Hashish, Hemp, Herb, Indian Hemp, Marijuana, Mary Jane, Pot, Red oil, Reefer, Smash, Stick, Tea, Thai stick and Weed) is one of the most widely used illegal drugs in the world. Between 41 and 47 million Americans are said to have tried cannabis and 16 to 20 million use it regularly. Despite its popularity it has also acquired a fairly evil reputation and usually seems to be associated with drugs such as heroin and cocaine. The truth is, however, that although many researchers have spent time and money investigating cannabis, and looking for problems associated with it, they have managed to find relatively few drawbacks to its use and no serious side effects or associated problems.

Action of cannabis

Cannabis heightens sensations such as touch, sound and smell, makes those who use it feel particularly relaxed and comfortable and occasionally produces hallucinations. But there is still no evidence to suggest that it is in any real sense of the word a 'dangerous' drug.

Technically a sedative and hypnotic drug, cannabis is commonly produced from the *Cannabis sativa* plant that grows easily and readily all over the world. The active ingredient is tetrahydrocannabinol, produced by the flowering tops and the leaves of the plant and most highly concentrated in the plant's resin. Marijuana is a mixture of the chopped leaves, stems and flowers of the cannabis plant that is prepared for smoking; charas or ganja is the unadulterated resin from the plant and is much stronger than marijuana. Hashish, also stronger than marijuana, is a powdered form of charas.

Early use

The cannabis story starts back in the 19th century. Cannabis was available in Britain and other Western countries where it had been used to help opium eaters kick their habit, but had never become particularly popular. The first scientific reports concerning the drug came from British doctors working in India, where cannabis had been widely used for many years, and from British doctors working at the Cairo Asylum in Egypt. The report which had the most impact was produced by Dr Warnock, Superintendent of the Cairo Asylum. It was he who, in 1895, suggested that cannabis might be a cause of insanity. It seems likely that he had come to this conclusion on the basis of the fact that many of the inmates of the asylum were enthusiastic cannabis users. He seems to have over-looked the fact that cannabis was extremely popular among people *outside* the asylum too.

Even at the time, Dr Warnock's point of view was not universally accepted. For example, the Indian Hemp Drugs Commission of 1893–4 was set up to examine the trade in hemp drugs, their effect on the social and moral condition of the people of India and the desirability of prohibiting their cultivation and use. The Commission's conclusion was that the physical, mental and moral effects of hemp drugs used in moderation were not adverse, that there was no evidence of cannabis use leading to addiction and that prohibition would be unworkable.

All the available evidence seemed to suggest that cannabis was no more damaging a drug than tea or coffee.

Introduction of legal controls

It was Dr Warnock's point of view rather than the Commission's report which had the greatest impact, however, when, in 1925 Britain, together with a number of other countries, signed the International Opium Convention. The Convention was designed to introduce binding international controls on the sale of opium and cannabis was included together with opium as a result of pressure from Egypt, where it was still believed that the regular use of cannabis could lead to mental problems. Britain and the other signatories accepted Egypt's request to include cannabis on the 'controlled' list since it seemed, at the time, to be a fairly modest concession. Doctors in Britain and other Western countries did not use cannabis and there was no large, Western commercial trade in the substance. The banning of cannabis, and its recognition as an addictive drug, seems to have been regarded as a small price to pay for persuading Egypt to sign a convention banning opium.

Repercussions of control

Ever since 1925, cannabis has remained on the 'controlled' drug list and legislators and police authorities have continued to harass cannabis users as well as cannabis smugglers. In Britain, for example, the 1971 Misuse of Drugs Act put cannabis into a class with the amphetamines (drugs which have been proved to be addictive) and ensured that cannabis users could face five years in prison, plus an unlimited fine.

This 60-year-old political bargaining has had important repercussions around the rest of the world, too.

In Nepal, for example, thousands of villagers have had their cannabis crops banned because of local laws which were brought in to conform with the international ruling. This has caused enormous problems in India and has led to much ill feeling. Cannabis is, after all, used in Hindu religious rites and is regarded as a 'holy' drug whereas alcohol, a drug frequently imported by those very Western officials who have over the years sought to see cannabis crops destroyed, is considered abhorrent by the Hindu people.

There have been similar problems in Jamaica, where cannabis has been used for well over one hundred years. Although cannabis was found growing in Jamaica in the late 18th century it seems to have been introduced into popular Jamaican culture in the mid 19th century by workers brought to the West Indies from India. Today ganja (the local name for cannabis) is used as a tonic, an energy source and a magical substance to ward off evil spirits. Its use in Jamaica seems to match very closely the usage described as common in India in 1894, when the Indian Hemp Drugs Commission reported. Some young middle-class Jamaicans have acquired their cannabis habit from America and Britain and use it as an aphrodisiac, or as a sign of teenage rebellion. But the traditional use is among rural agriculture workers who regard ganja as such an essential part of their daily diet that it is not unknown for ganja tea to be put into an infant feeding bottle.

The way these two social groups use cannabis in Jamaica illustrates quite vividly the way that one drug can have quite dissimilar effects when used in different circumstances, and confirms that the effects of a drug depend on circumstances and mental attitudes rather than solely on the pharmacology of the drug.

Those rural workers who use ganja in tea and tonics, who regard it as a medicine and an accepted, normal part of daily life, and who have high regard for its properties as an aid for the treatment of everything from colds to impotence, and from period pains to nerve troubles, rarely seem to develop any problems associated with the drug's use. On the other hand, the young middle-class Jamaicans who use cannabis as a social lubricant, purely for fun, are quite likely to run into trouble, to fail to turn up for work, to have problems at home and so on. The drug is then blamed and legal pressures on the rural workers are stepped up.

The heaviest users of cannabis in Jamaica are probably the Rastifarians who believe that the substance gives them divine powers. The Rastifarians are a black, messianic sect who wear their hair long and sport beards. They worship the late Haile Selassie and seek repatriation to Ethiopia as a major goal. There are now many thousands of Rastifarians in Jamaica and some in Britain. (There are many semi-Rastifarians or rastoids who adopt the hair style, the manners and the speech of the Rastifarians because they seek some sort of racial identity rather than because they believe in Haile Selassie or in repatriation to Ethiopia.) For Rastifarians, the legislation controlling cannabis is a nightmare. The penalties for possessing cannabis are a little higher than they used to be in Jamaica but for many Jamaicans laws controlling cannabis are about as logical as laws controlling communion wine might be to Christians.

The international controls on cannabis have had important repercussions in Britain and America, too. Because the drug is illegal many millions of ordinary, usually law abiding citizens have found themselves temporary members of an illegal subculture. The consequences of this are described at greater length later on but there are a couple of points that need making here.

First, because cannabis is clearly neither particularly dangerous nor addictive, linking it with heroin and cocaine has weakened respect for the laws which control those two drugs. The popular feeling is that since the risks associated with cannabis have been overemphasised then the risks associated with heroin have probably been overemphasised too.

The second major problem is that by forcing cannabis users underground, and into contact with black marketeers, the law has given heroin and cocaine dealers and pushers a large, often affluent, market to blackmail and to sell drugs to.

COCAINE

■ SIGNS OF ADDICTION

Cocaine users tend to be excitable and irritable. They may have hallucinations and they may complain of a 'crawling' sensation in their skin. Addicts who sniff or inhale will often have a runny nose.

Users tend to develop just one purpose in life – to obtain and use cocaine. They will abandon work, spend all their savings, leave families, lose friends and give up long established hobbies. They will sever (sometimes by neglect) long standing emotional and sexual relationships. They will probably be very secretive. They will lie and steal in order to obtain cocaine and will make promises that they cannot keep. Sleep patterns may be broken and they will very probably have severe money problems. They may eventually become scruffy, dirty and unkempt. They may also get into trouble with the law – for possession of cocaine, for trying to carry it through customs or for dealing in a small way.

■ LONG TERM POSSIBLE EFFECTS

Convulsions and depression. Damage to the lining of the nose, caused by regular sniffing, is common, as is lung damage. Cocaine users often lose their appetites and become emaciated. Serious health problems may develop after several years of apparently harmless use.

■ WITHDRAWAL EFFECTS

The cocaine user giving up his addiction will probably suffer from depression, tiredness and sleeplessness.

■ GIVING UP

Although many users believe that it isn't, cocaine *is* an addictive drug. Few family doctors are experienced in dealing with patients with this problem, and for medical help users will usually need to be referred to a specialist clinic. Although expert help is advisable, it is possible to withdraw from cocaine without expert help by resting quietly in a comfortable, relaxed, friendly atmosphere.

As with other types of addiction it is important to find out why the addiction began. If circumstances and pressures are not altered the addict is likely to begin using cocaine again soon after giving up.

See also pages 165–172 for general advice on helping an addict, emergencies, giving up and where to find help.

For the natives of Bolivia, Peru, Argentina and the hillsides of the Andes in South America, coca leaf chewing is a peaceful, harmless way of dealing with stress, pressure and a harsh, cruel environment. They started chewing coca leaves hundreds of years ago and never really ran into any trouble as a result of the habit.

To begin with the habit was confined to a fairly select few within the Inca empire; religious leaders and civic authorities being among the relatively small number of people allowed access to the leaves, and either chewing them or using them to make tea. But even when the Spanish conquerers of South America discovered the benefits of the leaves and encouraged the locals to use them more widely there were still no really dangerous side effects or unpleasant consequences. The Spanish simply used the leaves as a sort of local currency – paying mine workers with small bundles of coca leaves – and took full advantage of the fact that chewing the leaves produces a sense of well being that helps the user to forget the most uncomfortable and distressing local circumstances.

Dangerous and destructive refinement

It wasn't until European and North American scientists started refining coca leaves and turning them into more powerful drug forms that we managed to turn a fairly innocuous habit into a dangerous and destructive addiction.

Coca leaves had been introduced into Europe in the 19th century but they never really caught on, even though some doctors used the leaves as a tonic. A Corsican called Angelo Mariani did do rather well by blending coca leaves with fine wines and producing a potent mixture which he called Vin Mariani. He got enthusiastic endorsements from two popes, four kings and such lions of the French literary establishment as Jules Verne, Alexander Dumas and Emile Zola. It was only when cocaine was first extracted from the leaves, in about 1860, that the coca habit became popular in European society.

Sigmund Freud, the Austrian who helped to found the whole concept of psychiatry and psychoanalysis, was an enthusiastic user of cocaine. He used it to help morphine addicts but he also advocated it for the treatment of fatigue and nervousness. He used it himself, too, as did many other eminent Europeans.

In England in the mid 1880s, medical journals were crammed with enthusiastic stories of ways in which cocaine could be used. Many of papers on the subject appeared in the *British Medical Journal* and cocaine was advocated as a local anaesthetic and as a treatment for such varied disorders as cancer, hay fever, sea sickness and nymphomania. The new drug was recommended in *The Lancet* and appeared in a number of widely available patent medicines.

The world's most famous detective, Sherlock Holmes, was an enthusiastic user of cocaine, and although by the late 1890s Conan Doyle (Holme's creator, who also happened to be medically qualified) was allowing the good Dr Watson to become increasingly critical of his friend's habit, the early stories suggest that cocaine was fairly widely used as an antidote to boredom. During the same period in America many patent medicines containing cocaine were introduced. It was even possible to buy soft drinks which contained cocaine. The drug was both readily available and quite inexpensive.

Fall in demand
The use of cocaine fell off at the start of the 20th century, and there are several possible explanations. Laws were introduced to control its availability, and because it was difficult to get hold of the leaves the drug had always remained fairly expensive. Also, it may well be that although cocaine was written about very widely it was never really used by the great mass of people: it may well have been a drug that was always a favourite of the more literate, better educated classes. While it is true that the patent medicines were made widely available at more modest cost, they contained relatively small amounts of cocaine and their life expectation was firmly cut short when legislation was introduced.

For half a century or so, from the early part of the 20th century up until the late 1960s, cocaine use fell away dramatically. The only regular users were the Bolivian and Peruvian peasants who were still enthusiastically chewing their unrefined coca leaves.

Indeed, during the mid 20th century the coca leaf customs seem, if anything, to have strengthened in South America. Coca leaves were still used as payment for labour to workers in distant areas of Peru and Bolivia and coca leaves were widely used socially. It was the custom to pass leaves round at small gatherings and coca leaves were placed on the table for patrons of bars and clubs in small, hillside towns. In the Andes, coca leaf chewing was a socially acceptable habit which played the same sort of role as alcohol does in most of the Western so-called civilised world. The coca leaf was even used as a medicine in the hill towns – with a hot water infusion or coca leaf tea being used for a fairly wide range of mental and physical problems. As recently as 1980 the World Health Organization reported that there were some four million regular coca leaf chewers in South America, with about half the adult population of the central Andes being regular users.

Under these circumstances coca leaf causes hardly any problems at all. The usual response to the leaves is a feeling of well being, quiet and calm. Socially disruptive behaviour following coca leaf use is almost unknown.

When chewed or turned into 'herbal' tea coca leaves are both useful and extremely safe.

Consequences of illegal trafficking

Unfortunately for the South American natives the Western passion for cocaine returned to America in the late 1960s, and it returned with a vengeance. It is difficult to say for sure why cocaine suddenly became fashionable after such a long gap but the fact that the drug continued to be used by doctors as a local anaesthetic ensured that it remained available. It was probably that availability, allied to the shortage of heroin in the 1960s, that led to cocaine's revival.

This was unfortunate for the natives of Peru and Bolivia for, in the early 1970s, Bolivian farmers found that they could increase their income many times if, instead of selling the coca leaves that their bushes produced, they used the leaves to produce illegal coca sulfate paste for an international illegal drugs trade to sell in America.

The local coca leaf chewers then found themselves facing two quite separate problems.

First, there were no longer enough leaves to go round. Farmers who had previously prepared crops for home consumption were now selling most of their leaves to the illegal exporters.

Second, they suddenly found themselves being harassed by the authorities. Drug control agents from America had traced the supply of cocaine back to the hillsides of the Andes and official pressure from the United States had turned a long accepted local custom into an illegal activity.

A third problem also affected the people of South America as a direct result of what was going on in North America. The leaves grown by the South America farmers were converted into cocaine by a huge number of illegal, underground laboratories which had sprung up all over Bolivia. But eventually the amount of cocaine being produced exceeded the demands of the international market and there was a glut. The obvious place for dealers to sell this excess was on the home market so, during the 1970s, a major drug problem was born in the countries of the Andes. Dealers found that the locals were keen to buy cocaine for two reasons. First, they couldn't get hold of the leaves because the leaves were going to the laboratories. And second, as more and more towns in South America were modernised and dragged into the 20th century so the chewing of coca leaves began to be regarded as a rather primitive, out of date habit. The local inhabitants were much more enthusiastic about using cocaine since that drug was fashionable in America.

This change in the way that coca was used in South America has had a number of disturbing effects on the local population.

To start with, cocaine is more expensive to buy than raw leaves, because the industrial processes have to be paid for.

Second, whereas coca leaves were obtained quite legally and used according to well established cultural patterns, cocaine has to be obtained illegally and furtively and used in ways that follow no traditional patterns. The coca leaf user was an accepted member of society. The cocaine user is not so readily accepted and may find himself alienated and excluded from normal society.

Third, cocaine has far more powerful and damaging effects on the mind, body and behavioural patterns of the user than coca leaves have. The cocaine content of the dry leaves is 1 percent of their weight whereas the concentration in coca paste (a substance produced as part of the refining process) may reach 45 percent. Also, whereas coca leaves are natural and unadulterated and produce no harmful effects when chewed, the cocaine invariably contains toxic substances and using cocaine or smoking coca paste produces hallucinations, confusion, weight loss, insomnia, anxiety, tremor and irritation. It also causes users to neglect themselves. When snorted or sniffed, cocaine can damage the lining of the nasal passages. The drug can speed up the heart, increase body temperature and produce strange, crawly feelings in the skin. It is a very different proposition to the simple, old fashioned coca leaves.

So the overproduction of cocaine in the 1970s had a fearful effect on the health of the people of the Andes. But worse was to come. During the late 1970s and early 1980s the demand for cocaine in the United States continued to grow. As the number of people in America wanting cocaine rose, and the number of coca bushes and laboratories being destroyed by drug control agencies increased, so the price of the drug went up and up – providing additional problems for Bolivian and Peruvian native cocaine users.

How the smugglers operate

Today, despite the efforts of the police, the movement of cocaine is big business. Something like 200,000 acres are devoted to coca leaf growing in Peru and Bolivia and most of the cocaine that is produced goes first to Columbia where they don't actually grow very much coca leaf but where they do play a part in the refining process. They also prepare the cocaine for transportation to the United States. Very little money is made by the peasant farmers of Bolivia or Peru (although they are undoubtedly making more than they did when they sold their coca leaves directly to local buyers). The major profits go to Colombian smugglers, for whom cocaine has become a very big business.

America is still by far the largest consumer of cocaine with 22 million Americans said to have tried it and over 4 million Americans currently said to be using the drug. The methods used to transport cocaine into the United States have become more and more sophisticated over the last few years.

For a while one of the most popular techniques was to 'body pack' cocaine. Smugglers put cocaine into rubber packets (balloons, condoms or the fingers snipped off surgical gloves) and then swallowed anything up to a couple of hundred packets. The main danger with this technique was that if a packet burst open the smuggler would probably absorb a lethal dose. A number of smugglers did indeed die this way. Many considered the risk worthwhile, however, for the profits from just one smuggling trip could turn a penniless peasant into a rich man.

These days, although some cocaine is still smuggled by 'body-packers', most is smuggled across borders by aeroplane. According to United States government experts, some 40 percent of the cocaine used in America gets into the country in private planes. Sometimes the planes simply land in some quiet spot to unload their supplies. Sometimes a plane will just fly low and dump cocaine into a pre-arranged spot. The occasional smuggler is caught and a number of planes have been confiscated but the potential profits are so enormous that the big time smugglers can afford to lose planes quite regularly without their profits being eaten into.

How cocaine is used
In American society, cocaine (known to users as coke, C, candy, snow, flake, leaf, blow, happy dust, nose candy, Peru-

vian lady and white girl) is the champagne of addictive drugs. It has a much better image than heroin (usually regarded as a rather down market 'street' drug) or substances such as 'angel dust' (otherwise known as phencyclidine or PCP, which can be smoked, swallowed or sniffed and which can act as a stimulant, depressant or hallucinogenic; angel dust is an almost exclusively American drug which is popularly thought of as a drug for the down and outs and the unemployed). It is used by people in positions of power and authority and, since it is an expensive drug, invariably most popular among individuals who have plenty of money. It is fairly widely used by showbusiness stars, lawyers, accountants, company directors and doctors. It is not unknown for people to pay their accountant or their dentist not with a cheque but with a bag of cocaine. There is now even a market in America for gold gadgets designed specifically for cocaine users. Two thirds of cocaine users are male but in recent years the number of women taking cocaine has steadily increased. Many claim that they get better orgasms and sexual experiences with cocaine, some argue that it is an aphrodisiac. Undoubtedly, many have turned to cocaine as a replacement for Valium and the other benzodiazepines, mistakenly believing that it is a soft alternative.

The traditional way for users to take cocaine is either by injection or by sniffing through a straw or crisp, rolled up dollar bill or from a small gold spoon. To get the best from sniffing the user lays a razor thin line of cocaine across a piece of smooth glass or metal, closes one nostril and sniffs the line of cocaine through the clear nostril. Cocaine is soluble in water so that when it touches the moist membrane in the nose it dissolves and goes straight into the blood stream. It takes about five minutes to get a kick from inhaling cocaine and the pleasant effect lasts from 20–60 minutes. The damaging effects can be much more long lasting.

Today, however, an increasing number of cocaine users are turning to freebasing – a technique that is said to give cocaine users the ultimate high. Cocaine itself is a refined component of the coca leaf but to freebase you carry the refining process one step further and free the active drug from its base.

Freebasing was relatively rare until 1979, when shops in America began mass marketing cheap extraction kits for cocaine users.

Powerful and destructive effects

The danger is that although freebasing cocaine gives a quicker and better 'kick' it is much more dangerous and likely to produce powerful and destructive effects. One cocaine addict has described the risks of taking cocaine this way as 'jumping out of an aeroplane and not knowing whether or not your parachute is going to open.'

The physical effects produced by cocaine, even when it is freebased, are relatively innocuous. One of the commonest problems is formication, a condition in which the skin feels as though it is alive with fleas. Other physical effects are rare. The main problems are the effects that cocaine use has on the brain and the mind. Whereas heroin users may end up with a wracked and ruined body, cocaine users are more likely to go mad.

Under normal circumstances our responses to specific situations are produced by chemical changes in the brain which regulate our drive to eat, to make love and to run away when we are in danger. Cocaine seems to have a direct effect on the manufacture and use of those essential chemical message transmitters, with the result that the drug eventually dominates the regular user's basic drives. Keep on using cocaine and you won't be interested in sex (you may obtain sexual pleasure from taking cocaine but may be quite uninterested in sex with another partner), food, water or even preserving your own life: all you will be interested in will be obtaining more cocaine. Your brain will have become totally hooked on the drug. This type of addiction is obviously destructive and can ruin an individual's life.

Three of the leading American experts on cocaine are Dr Mark S Gold, director of research at Fair Oaks Hospital in Summit, New Jersey, who established the National Cocaine Hospital which took 400,000 phone call enquiries during its first year; Dr Ronald K Siegel, who recently spent nine years completing the first full scientific study of regular cocaine users; and Dr David E Smith, who founded the Haight-Ashbury Free Medical Clinic to treat drug victims. They all agree that cocaine is much more dangerous than we once thought, and that we still don't know just how it works or which users are most likely to develop problems from its use.

They are also agreed that cocaine is an addictive drug. Many users still believe that it is neither addictive nor particularly dangerous. All the evidence proves that they are wrong. Cocaine is addictive and it is a killer. So far its use has been largely restricted to the United States. The profits made out of the drug, and its social status, mean that it is likely to be a drug with a world wide market in the near future. American Under Secretary of State, Jon Thomas, estimated that ten tons of cocaine would be smuggled into Western Europe in 1985. Every time a film star is reported as using cocaine, the likelihood of the drug's use spreading increases.

GLUES AND OTHER SOLVENTS

■ SIGNS OF ADDICTION
The glue sniffer may appear drunk, his movement uncoordinated and speech slurred. He may suffer auditory and visual hallucinations, or experience blurred vision. His hair, breath or clothing may smell of solvents. There may be solvent stains on his clothes. He may lack appetite or suffer diarrhoea – either way he will lose weight. He may be moody and irritable. He may have a rash around his nose and mouth, a running nose and eyes, the general symptoms of a cold and a cough that persist for an unusually long time. Truancy from school or absenteeism from work are other common problems.

Glue sniffers tend to have just one purpose – obtaining and using the substance to which they are addicted. They will avoid non-using friends, show no interest in relatives, lose interest in long established hobbies and often sit around for long periods doing absolutely nothing. They are invariably secretive and may lie and steal in order to sustain their addiction. They make promises that they have no intention of keeping and often become untidy and dirty. Their sleep pattern may be disturbed. They may run into money problems and have trouble with the law as a result of trying to obtain supplies of the solvent they are using.

■ LONG TERM POSSIBLE EFFECTS
Glue sniffing can damage the heart, lungs, liver, kidneys and nervous system.

■ WITHDRAWAL EFFECTS
Glue sniffers giving up their drug may develop abdominal cramps, nausea, aching limbs, tiredness and depression. They may suffer from these symptoms for several days.

■ GIVING UP
If a glue sniffer has physical problems or needs to stay in hospital for investigation or support then medical help is clearly essential. Otherwise most doctors have little to offer glue sniffers.

As with other types of addiction it is important to find out why the addiction began. If circumstances and pressures are not altered the addict is likely to begin using glue again soon after giving up.

See pages 165–172 for general advice on helping an addict, emergencies, giving up and where to find help.

Glue, paint thinner, hair spray, cleaning fluid, lighter fluid, gasoline, liquid shoe polish, household metal cleaners and nail varnish all contain volatile vapours that can be sniffed or inhaled and used to produce a range of effects similar to those obtained with such powerful drugs as the barbiturates and the opiates. Most of the vapours produced by these substances are central nervous system depressants and produce intoxication, drowsiness, dizziness, hallucinations and a loss of consciousness.

Although the technique of inhaling vapours to produce a psychological effect goes back a long way – the Delphic Oracle of Ancient Greece did it – the modern craze for sniffing and inhaling seems to have first appeared in rural areas of America in the 1950s, when petrol sniffing was popular. The glue sniffing craze developed in the 1960s and in the last two decades has spread round the world. Today there are glue sniffers in America, Europe, Africa and Latin America. In some parts of the world, Mexico for example, glue inhalation is one of the major addiction problems.

Most glue sniffers are male and usually teenagers. Very occasionally the habit starts by accident – a boy may be making a model aeroplane when he finds out that he likes the smell of the glue – but in the vast majority of cases a youngster tries sniffing because it is the fashionable thing to do: his friends are doing it and he doesn't want to be left out. An additional, important advantage is that the substances involved are all relatively cheap and easy to obtain.

The sniffer will start with glue squeezed out of the tube onto a handkerchief or scrap of paper. Later on inhalation techniques become more sophisticated, with the users putting a small amount of their favourite substance into a small polythene bag or empty crisp bag and warming it in their hands to produce a good supply of vapour, which is then inhaled.

Effects of glue sniffing

After a few deep breaths the sniffer usually starts to feel dizzy but he will also feel unusually happy and may have a tremendous feeling of exhilaration. Experienced sniffers say it's the same sort of thrill that alcohol produces. He may experience hallucinations – seeing and hearing things that just aren't there – he may see double and he may feel nauseated and drowsy. After a few days or weeks of this sort of response the sniffer discovers that he needs more and more of his chosen substance to get the desired effect.

Apart from the psychological problems produced by the inhalation of addictive volatile solvents there are dangerous physical effects too. For example, these products can cause serious and irreversible damage to the brain, heart, liver, kidneys and nervous system. The bone marrow can be affected and so can the entire blood system. Disorientation, epileptic fits and sexual problems are common. Boys who have been sniffing for some time usually have little appetite so they are seriously underweight, listless, tired and moody. Deprived of essential nutrients their bodies are vulnerable to infection too.

Although the dangers associated with glue sniffing have been consistently underestimated, the truth is that glue sniffing can kill. Indeed, in *Drugs of Abuse: An Introduction To Their Actions and Potential Hazards* Dr Samuel Irwin ranks glue sniffing as more dangerous than using amphetamines, cigarettes, alcohol, barbiturates, heroin, and hallucinogens such as LSD or marijuana. In recent years there have been several reports of social workers and others trying to play down the risks associated with glue sniffing and assuring young sniffers that glue is relatively safe. Some doctors, school teachers and parents also regard glue sniffing as a minor problem. But the statistics show that glue sniffing has been responsible for a number of deaths and many cases of permanent physical damage.

One of the major difficulties for parents is the fact that by the time the young sniffer shows such clear symptoms as weight loss, moodiness, inattentiveness, drowsiness, un-usual irritability, tremor, persistent headaches, sores or rashes around his mouth or nose, running eyes and nose, a cough and the general symptoms of a cold that doesn't get any better (and solvent stains on his clothing) he is likely to be addicted. School work will be forgotten, chores ignored and if he is lucky enough to have a job that, too, will be relegated to a position of little importance.

To date, a great deal has been written about glue sniffing but little has been done to eradicate the problem. In Britain, for example, the Government has appealed to retailers and manufacturers to do what they can to prevent the sale of glues and other solvents to children and there has also been much talk about the responsibility of parents and police.

In the summer of 1983, John Patten, Parliamentary Secretary for Health, issued a press release designed to discourage glue sniffing. His appeal began, 'I would say to teenagers tempted to try it out – Don't do it. It's just not worth it.' He went on, 'To those who are already glue sniffing I would say – "If you find you can't stop, ask for help – go to your parents, teachers or youth leaders – some older person you can trust for help".' Mr Patten seems to have ignored the fact that when 12-year-old children are so miserable and lonely that they spend their free hours huddled underneath canal bridges trying to blow their minds and forget the real world by sniffing glue out of old crisp bags there is something drastically wrong and an appeal to 'pull up your socks and be a sensible fellow' isn't likely to change things very much.

Addiction to glue and other solvents seems likely to remain a significant problem for some time to come. It's certainly one that all parents should be aware of.

HEROIN, MORPHINE AND OPIUM
(also Diconal, Methadone, Pethidine)

■ SIGNS OF ADDICTION

The heroin user is likely to have very small pupils and little appetite. He may be aggressive and irritable and unable to sleep. He may sweat a good deal. If he is using the drug intravenously there will probably be tell-tale needle marks – usually where the veins can be reached easily. The most popular sites are the forearms, particularly in the inside bend of the elbow. When these veins get worn out by overuse addicts will turn elsewhere. Some addicts, aware that veins in the arms are the ones most commonly used (and inspected) try to avoid them. Addicts who have not used clean equipment or sterile injection techniques often have infected sores at injection sites. Addicts who sniff or inhale may have a runny nose and/or eyes. Heroin users tend to have bowel problems (such as constipation), general flu-like symptoms and a persistent tremor.

Addicts tend to have just one purpose – obtaining and using the drug to which they are addicted. This means that they probably aren't very interested in anything else. They will miss school or stay away from work, abandon friends and stop seeing relatives. They will end emotional and sexual relationships. They will give up long established hobbies and often sit around for long periods doing hardly anything.

They are usually secretive and dishonest. They will lie and steal, even from their nearest and dearest. They will make promises that they cannot and will not keep. They are often untidy, dirty and unkempt and they will almost invariably have money problems. They will commonly get into trouble with the law as a result of being in possession of drugs, stealing in order to buy drugs, soliciting in an attempt to raise essential cash or even selling drugs themselves.

■ LONG TERM POSSIBLE EFFECTS

The long term heroin user will be physically weak and debilitated. He will have lost weight and may have infections. He will probably be constipated.

■ WITHDRAWAL EFFECTS

The heroin user who gives up will have flu-like muscle pains, anxiety, headaches, diarrhoea, nausea, vomiting and general weakness for a few days.

■ GIVING UP

Few family doctors are experienced in dealing with patients who have this problem and for medical advice users will usually need to be referred to a specialist clinic. It is possible to withdraw from heroin without expert help by resting quietly and completely in a friendly, comfortable atmosphere. Simple pain-killers should be used for aches and pains. Warm baths and hot water bottles often help too. The difficulty of heroin withdrawal has been exaggerated in some films and books. In practice it is sometimes easier to give up heroin than it is to give up barbiturates or benzodiazepines.

It is important to find out why the addiction began, because if circumstances and pressures are not altered the addict is likely to begin using heroin again soon after giving up.

See pages 165–172 for general advice on helping an addict, emergencies, giving up and where to find help.

Heroin, morphine and opium are all narcotic drugs which are derived from the same basic source and produce similar effects on the people who take them. Extracted from the oriental poppy plant which grows in such varied places as India, Turkey, China, Russia, Egypt and Mexico these narcotics all depress the central nervous system, relieve pain, induce sleep, cure coughing and diarrhoea and can produce an extraordinary feeling of comfort and well-being. They make stress and worry fade away and create a warm feeling of euphoria.

The basic product obtained from the poppy plant – opium – is the dried juice from the plant's pods. When pods are cut open, white juice oozes out and quickly turns a deep reddish brown as it oxidises in the air, eventually hardening into balls of gum which have a sweet smell and a bitter taste.

Opium has been used for thousands of years. The ancient Greeks and Romans called it the 'destroyer of grief', while the ancient Egyptians used it for a variety of purposes – including quietening crying children. We tend to associate the opium poppy with the Far East but it wasn't until Arab merchants carried it there in the 1500s that the drug became popular in either China or India.

By the 17th century opium had reached most of Europe and Thomas Syndenham, one of the great fathers of English medicine and a renowned teacher and physician, recommended it for the treatment of pain and for helping patients to rest and sleep. British doctors didn't have many useful drugs available at the time and took to opium with tremendous enthusiasm. Within a century or so it was being wildly over used in England and one worried observer pointed out that its use to deal with hysterics and nervous disorders was like giving pills to try and 'purge folly'. Opium was to 18th-century England what Valium is to the world in the 20th century.

But it was in China that the opium drug caught on in a big way. The poppy plants grew there in great profusion so there was no shortage. By the 19th century the Chinese rulers had recognised the damage that the drug was doing and twice went to war with the British, whose trade domination of the Chinese mainland was closely linked to opium smuggling. The British won both wars, however, and in the mid 19th century the opium trade became legal. Those British victories and the legislation of the opium trade subsequently led to major problems around the world. For example, it was the legalisation of opium in China that led to its widespread use in the United States in the later part of the 19th century.

Fatal versatility

When we think of opium use in Britain we tend to think of it in association with writers such as Thomas de Quincey and Samuel Taylor Coleridge, both confessed opium addicts. We tend also to think of opium as one of the early 'recreational' drugs. That's a mistake. For the greater part of the 19th century opium was available at modest prices just about anywhere in the world; you could buy it either in local stores or by mail order. It was sold for a thousand and one different purposes. In huge areas of England it was sold over the counter without any restrictions, and was generally regarded as a useful home medicine. Indeed, De Quincey himself first started to use opium as a medication. Even after the drug was brought under legislative control in England, in 1868, it was still widely available and accepted socially as a useful, indeed vital, medicine. It was nowhere near as damaging as its derivative heroin – but it was nevertheless dangerous.

People used opium to help them sober up when they had been drinking too much and to help them cope with the appalling conditions brought about by the Industrial Revolution. Parents used opium to treat their children when they developed gastro-intestinal infections and diarrhoea from drinking foul, infected water. Poor water supplies, inadequate sewage facilities and terrible overcrowding caused thousands to suffer from disorders such as cholera. Doctors could not cure the medical problems, but opium did ease the pains, control diarrhoea and help people forget.

The use of opium in England was recognised as a problem in itself only when widespread use of the drug led to people dying from opium poisoning and from opium overdosage.

Ineffective control

Clearly, something needed to be done, and the medical and political authorities together forged the 1868 *Pharmacy Act* to control the sale of opium. However, not even legislation helped very much. During the mid 19th century physicians and apothecaries fought for power within the medical profession. As a result, the 1868 *Pharmacy Act* was deliberately kept weak. In practice, all the Act meant was that if you wanted to buy opium you had to buy it from someone with an officially accepted qualification. That didn't affect the numbers of people using opium: it just meant the profits relating to its sale were channelled into the hands of the medical and pharmaceutical professions. Opium could only be sold by a registered pharmacist and had to be labelled as a poison, but it could still be bought freely. It was a purely commercial victory.

The 1868 Act was weakened even further by the fact that pressure from patent medicine manufacturers ensured that patent medicines containing opium were excluded from the Act. (Some opium-rich products were still available over the counter, without a prescription, in the 1970s.)

During the 19th century three things happened which further complicated the whole issue.

1. A growing number of people started using morphine rather than opium. Morphine is a chemically refined version of opium and it has very similar qualities, but is 10 times as powerful as raw opium.

2. On November 28 1853, Alexander Wood gave the first hypodermic injection (of morphine) to an elderly spinster in Edinburgh. He used sherry as a solvent for the morphine on the grounds that it would be less likely than water to rust the syringe. Doctors quickly became enthusiastic about this new method of using an opium product and many claimed that it was safer than the old fashioned ways. As happens so often, doctors uncritically adopted a new technique (injection) and a new product (morphine) and by doing so created a bigger problem than there had been before.

3. Heroin was produced from morphine for the first time; heroin is approximately 20 to 25 times as powerful as morphine and twice as addictive. It has the classic bitter taste of opium but is quite odourless. In its pure state it is a greyish brown, but when diluted it becomes white. The main problem with heroin, as opposed to morphine or opium, is that the human body becomes very tolerant to it in a relatively short space of time and to get the same effect you have to take increasingly massive doses. Predictably, perhaps, when heroin was first introduced doctors welcomed it as a safe, non-addictive alternative to opium. (The pattern continued half a century later when methadone was introduced as a synthetic pain-killer said to be a safe, non-addictive alternative to heroin. Methadone is now known to be addictive and thousands of users are dependent on it.)

These three innovations ensured that the narcotics problem continued to get bigger. Belatedly, the politicians, lawyers and doctors got together to try to control what had become a massive international problem. In Britain, for example, a series of laws was introduced at the end of the 19th century and early in the 20th century in an attempt to control the use of these opiate drugs.

And the laws seemed to work. By the time the *Dangerous Drugs Act* was introduced in 1920 opium, morphine and heroin were being used far less frequently and the drug problem had been reduced quite dramatically. In retrospect, however, it is clear that the number of people using the drugs fell rapidly well before these laws were introduced. Social improvements which took place in British society in the latter part of the 19th century had removed the need for the drug. With social reformers such as Edwin Chadwick leading the way, Britain had built an impressive series of sewage works, water supplies and other public services. The incidence of diseases such as cholera fell away dramatically and the need for opiates disappeared as living standards improved.

However, around the rest of the world the use of opium, morphine and heroin was still escalating. An attempt was made to bring these drugs under control before the First World War but failed fairly miserably and it wasn't until 1925 that any real attempt was made to control the use of these drugs on an international scale. Things went slowly, however, and the start of the Second World War put an end to international co-operation. By the early 1950s, by which time the World Health Organization had been created, it was clear that the only real answer was to make heroin (the most concentrated, powerful, dangerous and profitable form of opium) totally illegal. It was argued that the drug had very limited uses in medicine and that making it completely illegal would reduce the supplies of the drug internationally, making it much easier for policing authorities to exterminate the drug completely.

This attempt to outlaw heroin was stopped by Britain's doctors who argued that its powerful pain-relieving qualities made heroin an essential drug. It could perhaps be argued that the world has the members of the British Medical Association to thank for its current heroin problem.

Professional and commercial pressures

This determination by British doctors to retain the right to prescribe at all costs subsequently led to our current explosion of heroin usage. Britain has now played a vital part in the continuing success of opiates on three separate occasions over the last century and a half. In the mid 19th century it was Britain who, for commercial reasons, encouraged the trade in opium throughout the Far East. In the early 1950s, it was Britain who refused to allow other countries throughout the world to outlaw heroin. And then in the 1960s it was again Britain who helped to create the current heroin problem.

In the 1960s, Britain – like many other countries – had a small, apparently controlled heroin problem. In a number of other countries the heroin problem was so desperate that doctors were only allowed to prescribe heroin if they had an official licence, or worked in special centres. In Britain, however, the medical profession insisted that it could deal with the problem without any legislative controls and that, wherever they happened to be practising, doctors should be allowed to prescribe heroin for addicts.

Unfortunately, this approach failed to take into account the greed and culpability of doctors, or the ability of addicts to lie convincingly.

Disastrous consequences

The result of this simplistic approach was absolutely disastrous for in the early 1960s all Britain's heroin addicts gravitated towards a very small number of doctors willing to prescribe for them. There were said to be no more than half a dozen doctors prescribing heroin for all Britain's addicts. Other doctors didn't want to get involved with patients who could be argumentative and troublesome.

The result was that Britain's small number of heroin addicts soon found themselves up to their knees in heroin supplies. In 1962, for example, one doctor prescribed almost 600,000 heroin tablets for addicts. On one occasion he prescribed 900 heroin tablets for a single addict. Three days later, he prescribed another 600 tablets for the same addict.

Two other doctors each signed prescriptions for over 1,000 tablets at a time. And nothing was done about it. The doctors could not be prosecuted because they were acting within the law. Their professional freedom to prescribe what they thought fit could not be questioned.

The British medical establishment had created a perfect situation for an illegal drug market. The heroin addicts who had excess supplies sold off what they didn't need and in order to create a profitable market for themselves encouraged their friends and neighbours to start using the drug.

(One of the classic ways of acquiring a drug market is to give away free supplies of an addictive drug to non-users. They use the free drug, get hooked and then have to pay for their supplies. In 1984, this technique was widely used by schoolboy pushers in Liverpool. Some would even argue that it was used even more profitably – albeit unwittingly – by Roche, the giant international manufacturer of tranquillisers, when it gave away supplies of Valium to British hospitals at a time when the British Government was worried about the cost of the drug to the National Health Service.)

Too late, doctors and politicians in Britain realised that they had made a mistake. In 1968 new regulations were introduced that made it necessary for doctors to notify drug addicts to the Home Office. A system of licensing for doctors was also introduced.

This meant that the addicts who had been created in the early 1960s by overprescribing were in difficulty. There was a shortage of heroin and the scene was set for the black market to develop into a truly profitable operation. The increased number of addicts and the shortage of heroin made it possible for the drug smugglers to keep their prices high.

If the British medical establishment had sat down and worked out a way to create an illegal drug culture in Britain they couldn't have done it more efficiently. And these bad decisions in Britain have undoubtedly had an effect on the rest of the world too. For as the black marketeers have grown stronger in Britain, so they have been better equipped to sell their drugs to the rest of the world. As the demand in Britain has grown so the success of the opium growers in the Far East has enabled them to increase the size of the problems there, too.

Reasons for heroin boom

Today, heroin is an international currency that is used by terrorists as well as crooks. There are huge profits to be made in this thriving, multi-million-pound international business. Most of the opium is produced in the 'Golden Triangle', which consists of Thailand, Burma and Lao Peoples Democratic Republic. The raw opium may be converted into morphine base in the Middle East, then turned into heroin in French and Italian laboratories. The drug is then probably carried around the world by the Mafia. Heroin is now sold in many countries, but particularly in Australia, Burma, Canada, Germany, Hong Kong, Italy, Malaysia, Singapore, Sweden, Thailand, the United Kingdom, the United States of America and Vietnam. Most heroin users are young people living in major cities. They may smoke it or inject it; either way, they are addicted.

The number of addicts has grown in the 1980s for several reasons.

1. The pushers are often very persuasive. Unlike the people selling tobacco and alcohol they cannot use sophisticated advertising techniques to sell their product. Instead, they use fear and terror. The underworld connections mean that addicts are often too frightened of what will happen to them to stop buying the drug they are using.

2. More importantly, economic and political changes in Iran, Pakistan and Afghanistan caused the price of opium to fall during the early 1980s. The cost of the raw opium has never been particularly high. The lower it falls, the greater the profits from turning it into heroin.

3. The number of addicts grows because those who are already hooked have to turn to crime in order to raise cash to pay for their habits. Some try thieving or prostitution. But most discover that the easiest way to raise money is to start dealing and pushing the drug to which they themselves are addicted. That, of course, means creating new addicts. If you are a pusher you can't go around selling to someone else's addicts if you want to stay alive. The easier it is to get hold of supplies (and the cheaper the supplies become) the easier it becomes for pushers to give away 'free' samples to potential new customers.

4. In areas where unemployment is a major problem, boredom and depression have led many young people to experiment with drugs such as heroin simply to relieve the monotony of a dull existence and to add excitement to a life with no hope. Today too many youngsters feel that they have nothing to lose by experimenting with drugs.

How heroin is used

The traditional way to use heroin has been to inject it straight into a vein (a technique known as mainlining), or into the skin (known as skin popping), but because addicts frequently use dirty syringes and needles, and rarely bother with sterile techniques when injecting themselves, both these methods are associated with a high incidence of infection. Hepatitis, for example, is an extremely common problem among heroin addicts who inject their drug.

Partly to avoid these problems of infection and partly because they erroneously believe that snorting, sniffing or inhaling heroin is safer and less likely to lead to addiction, a growing number of heroin users are taking their drug this way. One of the most popular techniques currently used is to heat the heroin and then inhale the smoke that is produced – a technique known as 'chasing the dragon'.

There are also some synthetic narcotics derived from petroleum products or coal tar. These artificial opiate-like drugs, which can be taken by mouth in tablet form, are addictive. Invented only for prescription use, these tablets find their way on to the black market. (Incidentally, in 1985, police in California reported that a black market drug 'designer' was producing and selling synthetic heroin look-alikes which act like the real thing but are up to 1,000 times as powerful.)

Effects of heroin

The risks associated with the use of heroin are many and varied. Addicts tend to neglect themselves and dedicate their lives to the search for fresh supplies. They tend to suffer from constipation and constant sleepiness. They usually lose huge amounts of weight. They run the risk of overdosing or poisoning themselves because there is never any way of telling just how pure a batch of heroin may be – nor of telling what impurities it may contain.

If a pregnant woman becomes addicted, it is quite likely that she will give birth to an addicted baby. The baby addict will tear at its skin, vomit, convulse and produce a heart-rending, high-pitched scream. Half the children born to mothers hooked on heroin are taken into care because their mothers just cannot look after them. Some are smothered or drowned by their parents.

Coming off heroin can be hazardous and extremely unpleasant (although, as I have already explained, the risks and problems have been exaggerated). Without his drug the heroin addict will usually develop all the symptoms of flu: chills, nausea, vomiting, sweating and muscular pains. He's also likely to suffer a great deal from anxiety.

The final irony in the heroin story is that although heroin is the drug that we in the West have grown to fear there are many parts of the world where opium is still smoked or eaten for medical as well as social reasons. In Afghanistan, Burma, Bangladesh, Egypt, Indonesia, Iran and other parts of the Middle East and south east Asia opium is frequently the only medicine available. In some of those countries opium has been an essential medical supply for centuries.

Opium itself is a potentially dangerous drug but, as the British discovered in the 19th century, it has its uses and advantages. In those countries where opium is still used, the tragedy is that the current international campaign against the use of the opiates annually reduces the amount of opium available. And with increasing amounts of the available opium being converted into heroin, the quantity available for raw, traditional use is constantly diminishing.

The result is that in countries such as Burma, Thailand and Malaysia the traditional use of opium has now been replaced by the use of the much more destructive heroin. As with coca leaves, the developed countries of the world have managed to replace a natural, traditional and relatively harmless habit with a more modern, dangerous and expensive habit.

All the signs suggest that the size of the heroin problem has still not reached its peak.

LSD AND HALLUCINOGENS
(also Mescaline and Psilocybin)

■ SIGNS OF ADDICTION
Users may suffer from hallucinations which persist long after the drug use has stopped. Sleep disorders are also common. Users may experience dizziness, nausea, sweats and anxiety. Headaches and tremors can also occur. Money problems may occur occasionally. LSD users often get into trouble with the law for possession of the drug.

■ LONG TERM POSSIBLE EFFECTS
LSD and the other hallucinogens can produce panic states and long-term psychological problems in some users. A 'flashback' experience can occur as late as six months after taking the drug – this may be fleeting but can last for some time.

■ WITHDRAWAL EFFECTS
LSD is not addictive, so there are not usually any withdrawal effects.

■ GIVING UP
To give up LSD the user simply needs to stop using it. The

hallucinogenic drugs are not addictive and withdrawal does not usually produce any special problems.

LSD (short for d lysergic acid diethylamide 25) is probably the best known hallucinogenic drug, but there are many others, some of which occur quite naturally, unlike LSD which is made synthetically in the laboratory. For example, there is mescaline which is obtained from a particular variety of spineless cactus plant native to Mexico and certain areas of southwestern United States. And there is psilocybin, another variety of natural hallucinogenic, obtained from a type of mushroom which grows quite easily in many parts of the world. Two of the other well known synthetic hallucinogens are STP (the letters stand for serenity, tranquillity and peace) and DOM (the DOM stands for the chemical formula of the drug: 2,5 dimethoxy-4-methylamphetamine). Incidentally, although the synthetic hallucinogenics are controlled drugs, the naturally occurring ones are not legally controlled: if you find a 'magic' mushroom then you can eat it or sell it quite legally (although if you find one that happens to be poisonous, it may kill you).

LSD and the other hallucinogens were very popular in the 1960s and 1970s but there always was and still is a good deal of mystery and confusion about just how they work and what they do. They certainly do trigger off all sorts of unusual mental effects. They affect the way that we appreciate and use our senses, for example. Colours seem much brighter under the influence of hallucinogenic drugs. A piece of fabric or a painting can appear dazzlingly bright. Touch and hearing are also affected – the ticking of a clock can suddenly be unbearably loud. The normal pattern of thinking goes too, visual and auditory hallucinations are common, repressed feelings and fears are released, and normal social inhibitions disappear. Users have died because of hallucinations. For example, users believing that they could fly have leapt off tall buildings.

Effects of hallucinogens

The main danger with these drugs is that because they have an effect on the mind, and because they affect the personality, they can produce serious mental problems.

In *Drugs – medical, psychological and social facts*, published by Penguin in 1967, Peter Laurie wrote: 'The illicit user is unlikely to take the drug in the company of people who understand what is happening to him and are willing to reassure him about it. It is as if someone dressed him in a diving suit and threw him into deep water without telling him how to work the valves. Even in clinical settings the outcome of the drug experience can be uncertain.'

Strictly speaking, LSD and other hallucinogenic drugs are not addictive drugs. Having said that, I suppose it is possible that if an individual took one of these drugs in order to escape from the real world and found that he preferred the new world, then he might get hooked on the drug. However, this is rather different to the usual psychological or physical addiction produced by the other substances dealt with in this book.

Reasons for decline in use

These days hallucinogenic drugs are very much out of fashion and rarely used. There are several possible explanations for this fall from favour.

1. The side effects and dangers associated with the hallucinogenic drugs were discussed at enormous length in the press and on television at the time when the drugs were most fashionable in the psychedelic sixties. The side effects and dangers were, in fact, greatly exaggerated but many would-be users were undoubtedly frightened off by the publicity.

2. The drugs were never widely prescribed, although some psychiatrists claimed they were useful for examining the minds of their patients, so there was never a steady supply of medically produced users. Nor were there large supplies of any hallucinogenic drug produced by a major company. (If a drug company had been able to find a use for one of the hallucinogenic drugs then the whole history of this group of drugs would have undoubtedly been quite different.)

3. Because the hallucinogens are not addictive the profits to be made by black marketeers are not particularly rewarding. You're much more likely to make money when people *have* to buy the product you are selling. There are still small 'factories' making LSD but the sales potential is much smaller than for amphetamines, cocaine and heroin.

TOBACCO

■ SIGNS OF ADDICTION
The regular user may have a reduced appetite, smell typically of tobacco and have nicotine-stained fingers. A cough is also common. Those who smoke in the evening may have difficulty in getting to sleep at night since nicotine can stimulate. Young tobacco users may lie to cover up their habit. Tobacco is expensive and money problems can be considerable. Children may steal to sustain a 'habit'.

■ LONG TERM POSSIBLE EFFECTS
Tobacco can cause lung cancer, circulatory problems, heart disease, stomach problems, asthma, bronchitis and sinus problems. Some people find that tobacco is a relaxant, others that it is a stimulant. It can produce a rise in blood pressure, a faster pulse and diarrhoea. Nicotine poisoning is an additional, occasional problem. The early symptoms include: abdominal pain, vomiting, headaches, sweating, dizziness and general weakness. Pregnant women who smoke are likely to give birth to small, sickly babies, and miscarriages are more common. Children whose parents smoke are likely to get more colds and chest infections than other children – they are also more likely to end up misusing drugs.

■ WITHDRAWAL EFFECTS
These depend on the effect that the user sought and

enjoyed. So, for example, someone who smoked to help him relax may suffer stress symptoms on giving up tobacco. Individuals who use cigarettes to keep their fingers occupied when nervous may start eating more – and putting on weight – when they give up smoking. Tiredness and irritability are two other common withdrawal symptoms.

■ GIVING UP

There are many recommended techniques for giving up smoking. When they are enthusiastic, family doctors can be a tremendous help, offering both support and advice. A few prescribe nicotine gum which sometimes helps smokers give up.

Hypnotherapists and acupuncturists claim to be able to help smokers wishing to break their habits. The evidence, however, suggests that these 'alternative' professionals are unlikely to be particularly successful. The smoker who really wants to give up smoking will be just as successful by himself as long as he follows a system of simple incentive.

I suggest that the smoker anxious to give up makes a list of all the places where he smokes, putting the place where he smokes most at the top of his list, and the place where he smokes least at the bottom. He should then give up smoking in each place in turn, starting at the bottom and working his way up the list at his own pace.

The smoker who uses cigarettes (or any other form of tobacco) to help him relax can help himself by learning alternative relaxation techniques. Most smokers will be able to augment this technique by counting the advantages of giving up smoking: they will save considerable amounts of money; their health will improve; they will set a better example to their children; they will have an improved life expectation; they will enjoy food more; and they will have better breath and cleaner teeth.

For general advice, see pages 165–172.

The smoking habit is said to have started when Christopher Columbus received a gift of tobacco leaves from the natives of San Salvador and brought them back to Europe. Throughout the 17th century tobacco gradually grew in popularity, mainly as a medicine that could be relied upon to cure just about anything from deafness to headaches to flushes. To begin with most people chewed tobacco; the idea of smoking the leaves was popularised by the Turks during the Crimean War.

By the end of the 19th century there were roughly equal numbers of people chewing and smoking tobacco in both Britain and America but the production of the first machine-rolled cigarettes revolutionised tobacco habits throughout the world. By the end of the First World War in 1918 (during which, incidentally, the British army distributed cigarettes to its own soldiers, thereby probably doing as much harm to its own men as the German army was doing), more people were smoking than chewing and cigarettes had overtaken pipes in popularity. The introduction of machine-rolled cigarettes had one other effect – women started smoking.

Once fairly large numbers of people started smoking tobacco it quickly became clear that some were getting addicted. In the 1890s there were already small companies selling products such as NO-TO-BAC to help smokers give up the habit.

Effects of smoking

As tobacco rose in popularity many scientists around the world started to investigate its properties – tobacco is one of the addictive drugs that has been particularly well researched. Way back in 1928 researchers isolated nicotine and identified it as an active ingredient of tobacco. They also found that it was a particularly poisonous substance: there is enough nicotine in the average cigar to kill two people. The only reason why cigars and cigarettes aren't instantly lethal is that the nicotine they contain is taken into the body fairly slowly. In a special issue of the *Journal of the American Medical Association*, William Pollin, the director of the US National

Institute of Drug Abuse, reported that nicotine is six or eight times more addictive than alcohol and Dr Jack Henningfield of NIDA's Addiction Research Centre claimed that nicotine is between five and ten times as potent as cocaine.

Apart from its poisonous qualities, nicotine has a number of undesirable effects on the body. It stimulates the central nervous system and increases the electrical activity of the brain, lowers the skin temperature, causes blood vessels in the skin to become narrow, increases the blood pressure and the heart rate and numbs the taste buds.

Cigarette smoke also contains other poisonous substances: for example, carbon monoxide gas. This reduces the oxygen-carrying capacity of the blood and is one of the main reasons why heavy smokers so often complain of a shortness of breath. Other chemicals contained in tobacco cause cancer.

Chewing tobacco leaves isn't particularly good for you but neither is it particularly lethal. The cigarette is a perfect example of how science and industry have together turned a relatively harmless pastime into an addiction. Modern cigarettes are perfectly designed to ensure that dangerous substances are directed into the body quickly, repeatedly and conveniently.

The list of diseases associated with tobacco smoking seems to grow annually. To begin with there are the respiratory disorders such as asthma and bronchitis. Chest infections are particularly common among smokers. Sinus troubles such as sinusitis and catarrh are also caused or made worse by tobacco, as are many gum and tooth disorders. Of the problems which affect the stomach, indigestion, gastritis and peptic ulcers have all been identified as being exacerbated by smoking. Many circulatory problems, raised blood pressure, arterial blockages and strokes are all known to be tobacco related. There is a strong link between smoking and heart disease. Finally, there is lung cancer, the disease perhaps most commonly associated with cigarettes.

According to official statistics, the majority of the thousands of people who have major surgery in Britain are smokers, 95 percent of all patients with serious arterial disease of the legs are smokers and it has been estimated that 20 percent of the 180,000 people who died of coronary artery disease in 1981 did so because they smoked. In 1984, the Chief Medical Officer at the Department of Health and Social Security in Britain reported that smoking is 'by far the largest avoidable hazard to health in Britain today and causes about 100,000 deaths in the UK each year.' A previous Chief Medical Officer at the DHSS once described the cigarette as 'the most lethal instrument devised by man for peaceful use'.

Dr Michael Russell of the Addiction Research Unit at the Institute of Psychiatry in London has even pointed out that exhaled cigarette smoke could kill as many as 1,000 non-smokers every year.

In America, the United States Surgeon General claims that tobacco is responsible for 340,000 deaths every year and the cost to American society, in terms of health care and lost production, was in 1982 estimated at nearly 40 billion dollars a year. Nor are the health problems the only troubles caused by smoking. For example, it has been estimated that 25 per-cent of all the fires which take place in America are caused by smoking.

Despite all this well documented evidence, countless mil-lions round the world are still regular smokers. Some of them start to smoke because they find that tobacco relaxes them; some because they find that tobacco stimulates them; some because it is the sociable thing to do.

But most of them continue to smoke because they become addicted to tobacco.

There has been much argument about whether or not people do get addicted to tobacco but it has been shown that if individuals are given low nicotine cigarettes to replace their normal brand they will tend to smoke more of the low nicotine cigarettes. This evidence seems to support the theory that smokers can become addicted to nicotine, tobacco and cigarettes.

It has also been shown that when individuals give up the tobacco habit they often suffer from withdrawal symptoms such as anxiety, restlessness and insomnia.

It is difficult, if not impossible, to say just which smokers are addicted to tobacco. But as a general rule anyone who smokes more than 20 a day, who lights up first thing in the morning or who cannot go for long without a cigarette without feeling rather 'odd' is an addict.

Attempts to control smoking

It has been known for many years that tobacco smoking causes health problems. And for a long time there have been those who object to cigarettes on the grounds that they are dirty and unpleasant. It is perhaps not surprising, therefore, that for a long time now people have been trying to stamp out the habit completely.

In Russia and Persia in the 17th century tobacco smoking was punishable by death. The Turkish Sultan Murad IV is said to have executed as many as 18 smokers a day. There was a ban on smoking in the streets in Prussia in the mid 19th century. And an 18th-century Swiss law imposed particularly heavy levies on smokers in an attempt to stamp out the habit.

One of the most vociferous opponents of tobacco smoking was probably King James I. In 1604, he wrote what was probably the first anti-smoking tract, called *A Counterblast to Tobacco*. It concluded that smoking is 'a custom loathsome to the eye, hateful to the nose, harmful to the brain, dangerous to the lungs, and in the black stinking fumes thereof, nearest resembling the horrible Stygian smoke of the pit that is bottomless.' He put up taxes in an attempt to control the habit.

Since tobacco smoking grew to epidemic proportions during the first part of this century, doctors, health educators and politicians have struggled to control the habit. They've tried just about every possible avenue. Meanwhile, those who are worried about the damage smokers are doing to their own health have been joined by many thousands who object to being enveloped in other people's cigarette smoke and who justifiably argue that the health of the non-smoker can be damaged by side stream or second-hand smoke.

In Israel, a woman who smoked on a bus was sent to prison

after passengers had complained; while a bus driver who blew cigarette smoke at a passenger who complained about him convicted of assault on the grounds that cigarette smoke is a dangerous weapon. It will only be a matter of time before the anti-smokers start sueing smokers who pollute the air in restaurants and offices. (The most vociferous opponents of smoking tend to be former smokers who have given up and who, like newly accepted members of the Catholic Church, tend to be evangelical and puritanical.)

Publicity for and against

Despite all the publicity about the dangers of cigarette smoking and the protests from those who object to the pollution of the atmosphere, the number of people smoking remains surprisingly high. Concerted anti-smoking campaigns occasionally win encouraging numbers of recruits but, although there has been a reduction in the number of smokers, the long-term battle against smoking seems to be having remarkably little effect. One reason for this is undoubtedly the skill with which the large tobacco companies plan their marketing campaigns and promote their products. For every 10 people who give up smoking, eight or nine non-smokers seem to take up the habit.

In Britain the tobacco industry still spends over £100 million a year on advertising and sponsorship, and although the British Government banned cigarette advertising on television in 1965 the industry's promotional activities have proved remarkably successful.

The argument from the tobacco industry and its clients in the world of advertising is that such publicity does not attract new smokers but merely persuades smokers to change brands. In 1981 the Advertising Association in Britain published a booklet entitled *Advertising and Cigarette Consumption*, written by M J Waterson, research director of the Advertising Association.

Waterson claimed that advertising expenditure has not had any significant influence on the total size of the cigarette market over the previous 20 years and claimed that 'advertising does not stimulate or maintain cigarette consumption levels'. How he could possibly know how many people would have given up smoking without there being any advertising I can't imagine. He concludes that 'a cigarette advertising ban would be both futile and damaging to the interests of the consumer'.

The World Health Organization's Expert Committee on Smoking Control Strategies in Developing Countries found this argument unconvincing. In 1982 it reported that 'some pro-smoking advertisements do not even mention a brand name', and that 'tobacco companies enjoying a complete monopoly in a country none the less advertise'.

That seems to destroy the Advertising Association's argument quite effectively and suggests that more controls on advertising would lead to a drop in the number of people smoking. (I deal with this aspect of tobacco control in more detail on page 113.)

Why controls are ineffective

The international tobacco lobby is a powerful one and many governments have been unwilling to take on the tobacco industry.

In Britain, for example, despite the fact that just about every investigating committee has concluded that controls on tobacco promotion need to be introduced through tough Government legislation, in 1982 the British Government announced – with some pride – that it had formed a new agreement with the Tobacco Advisory Council and the Imported Tobacco Products Advisory Council.

The new agreement, covering such vital subjects as the presentation of Government Health warnings on cigarette packets is about as restrictive as a piece of cotton around an elephant's legs. It seems unlikely to have any effect on the numbers of people smoking in Britain. Shortly before the agreement was made the World Health Organization's experts concluded that the effect of a ban on tobacco promotion depends not only on the absence of advertising but also on the impact of a government's decision to act. 'A decision to ban tobacco promotion helps to create a climate in which . . . health education can flourish, free of sophisticated, expensive and misleading opposition', they decided.

Those wondering how the tobacco industry could persuade the British Government to accept such a hollow agreement should remember that the tobacco industry pays something like £4000 million a year in tobacco taxes alone, and that a number of politicians have close links with the industry. Amazingly, 6 percent of the British Government's revenue comes from the tobacco industry.

In an attempt to give the agreement a more acceptable look, the Government and tobacco industry announced (at the same time as they announced their voluntary controls on advertising) that the tobacco industry was giving £11 million for research into 'means of encouraging people, especially the young, to adopt a more responsible attitude to promoting and maintaining their own health' and investigating 'environmental, social and other factors which might affect the achievement of a more responsible attitude to good health.' The snag was that the £11 million was not to be used for anything to do with tobacco, and many doctors in Britain quickly refused to have anything to do with the research trust that was set up with the money.

Other countries have been braver and have taken on the tobacco industry – with considerable success. A study of smoking in 15 countries, published in the British Government's own official journal *Health Trends*, recently concluded that 'the countries which have evolved the most stringent anti-smoking policies (such as Norway and Finland) are among the lowest consumers of tobacco'.

The irony is that the report in *Health Trends* concluded that 'measures that attempt to decrease smoking (through a ban on advertising or smoking in public places and so on), may prove to be more important in smoking control than some of the efforts directed towards individual health education.'

It is difficult to avoid the conclusion that the British Government's determination to stick to voluntary agreements with the tobacco industry is a result of pressure from the industry. Just what sort of pressure it is impossible to say but it is difficult to believe that money is not involved.

Apart from controlling advertising and promotions there are several other ways in which governments *can* control the amount of tobacco being smoked. The most obvious technique is to increase the amount of tax on tobacco. When King James I published his treatise on smoking, he put up tobacco import taxes by a hefty 4,000 percent in a successful attempt to control the spread of the habit. But few governments seem prepared to take the risk of putting up taxes and losing revenue.

The simple, rather sad, fact is that although there have been political, economical, social, medical and educational attempts to control smoking, it is too widespread a habit to be made totally illegal. And the amount of money involved is too great for governments to be able to control the companies involved.

Smoking in Britain is now a minority habit (in that slightly less than half the population now smoke) for the first time since 1945. But the anti-smoking campaign seems unlikely to make further progress. Indeed the tobacco industry seems to be doing very well at the moment. British-American Tobacco Industries PLC had a 45 percent gain in pretax profits for the first half of 1984.

Recruiting new addicts

Not that the tobacco companies would go to the wall even if the Government did introduce a ban on all advertising and a considerable rise in tobacco taxes. The industry has proved itself extremely adept at planning for its own healthy future. For example, as older smokers have given up the habit so the tobacco industry has been very successful in persuading more youngsters to start the habit (this again belies the claim from the Advertising Association that advertisements only persuade people to switch brands). In Japan, tobacco companies have produced four different flavours of candy-flavoured filter cigarettes especially to attract young smokers while, according to recent figures published by the World

Health Organisation, nearly 50 percent of all teenagers leaving school already smoke. In America, chewing tobacco and snuff have become incredibly popular with children, thanks to a series of powerful promotional campaigns featuring sports stars.

However, the tobacco industry's greatest growth area has been the developing countries. The major companies started to move into developing countries some time ago and have been remarkably successful there for a number of reasons.

1. Most ironical of all, in many developing countries pressure from the Western, so-called civilised, countries has often led to the disappearance or control of long established, traditional drugs such as coca leaf or cannabis. The tobacco, alcohol and tranquilliser producing industries must welcome this clamp down with tremendous enthusiasm – every move towards controlling such traditional products opens up a new market for the world's biggest drugs of addiction. In China, where the use of opium is now frowned on, about 25 percent of the population smokes cigarettes regularly. That is another 250 million customers for the tobacco industry.

2. Developing countries have been unable to resist the temptations offered by the tobacco companies. When moving into a new country, tobacco companies offer a complete and apparently sound economic package. They teach local farmers how to grow tobacco, put up money for manufacturing centres to turn the raw leaf into cigarettes, and sell and promote the product internally. They sometimes offer irresistible profit opportunities to local leaders. And they inspire those politicians who resist personal temptations by talking about export profits and overseas currencies. Once a developing country is caught in the tobacco trap it is extremely difficult to escape, for the simple but important reason that the country's economy will have become tobacco based.

3. The consumption of tobacco in developing countries rises rapidly once the tobacco companies move in for the very simple reason that the advertising campaigns that are organised are not usually regulated in any way. The controls on tobacco advertising in Britain are feeble enough, but those on advertising in developing countries are usually non-existent. There are neither government regulations nor anti-smoking messages to counter the promises made by the advertisers.

Tobacco products can be advertised with messages associating tobacco with educational, financial and personal success, with good health, and sexual strengths and powers. Cigarettes can usually be marketed without any warnings and with a much higher tar content than is allowed in most developed countries.

By the time the developing country's government realises that its health bills are rocketing (and probably exceeding the revenue in taxes) and the medical profession is aware of the rapidly rising problem, huge numbers of the population will be well and truly hooked. The tobacco company will have acquired another market of addicted customers. Throughout the 1970s the consumption of tobacco in developed countries fluctuated around the annual figure of 2Kg per person. Developing countries around the world currently show annual consumption levels to be around 0.8Kg per person but the figure in those parts of the world is rapidly rising.

As each developing country emerges from poverty and obscurity the first people to take advantage of the growing affluence will be the tobacco companies. They make the Mafia and the Colombian cocaine runners look like badly organised charity groups. And by the time a government realises what has happened it will be hooked on the tobacco industry's money just as surely as its inhabitants will be hooked on the industry's products.

In Brazil, for example, the cigarette industry has become the largest taxpayer. Brazil has the highest tobacco tax in the world, with 75 percent of the retail price of a cigarette going to the Government, but because of this high tax rate 11.6 percent of Brazil's revenue comes from the tobacco industry. During the first five months of 1983 the Brazilian Government collected over $500 million from taxes on cigarette sales.

Small wonder then that the Brazilian Government can only sit and watch with horror as the number of people suffering from disease caused by cigarettes rockets. Smoking is now Brazil's major cause of death and disease: over 20,000 people a year die of heart disease and another 20,000 die of cancer – all caused by tobacco. Smoking is now the single most important factor producing perinatal mortality and infant mortality. In a country where poverty and inflation are major problems, the tobacco industry is cleaning up.

All this financial return for the marketing skills and bargaining agility of the tobacco industry should be more than enough. But the success of the industry in the developed countries is further assisted by the fact that in 1984 the European Economic Community's Agricultural Policy gave European tobacco farmers a $667 million subsidy. That means that every tax payer in Europe is helping to support the world's richest and most successful industry of addiction.

OTHER PRESCRIPTION DRUGS

I doubt if there has ever been a prescription drug to which a patient somewhere has not become addicted. The problem is that when a physician hands a patient a prescription the deed is charged with many different feelings and forces. Naturally, the patient wants to get better. He will respond to the physician's attitudes and feelings almost as much as he will respond to the drug. And he may well misinterpret the function of the drug or the physician's purpose in prescribing it. The patient may well come to believe that the drug has qualities it does not possess, responding to his own imagination rather than to the pharmacological qualities of the drug. But it is to the drug that he will become addicted.

It is possible for a patient to become addicted to a drug if he believes that the drug will help prevent him having a heart attack. Similarly, a patient may get hooked on antibiotics if he believes that by taking them he will avoid contracting any dangerous or debilitating infection.

Sometimes this simple type of psychological addiction may be combined with a vital physical addiction. That can cause danger as well as confusion. Consider a patient who is taking a corticosteroid drug for the treatment of asthma. The drug will have a dramatic effect on the patient's condition and he is quite likely to become dependent on the drug. He will be reluctant to stop taking the tablets because he will fear that without them his asthma may return. In addition to that psychological addiction, however, the drug may induce a physical addiction. Corticosteroids, when taken in drug form, depress the body's ability to produce its own natural supply of steroids. That means that if the corticosteroids are taken for long enough then the body can become truly, physically dependent on a continuing supply of the drug. Most doctors take care to ensure that they only allow their patients to take steroid drugs for a few days at a time but millions of asthmatics, arthritics – and sportsmen – have become doubly addicted in this way.

Of the other prescription drugs that are addictive, hormone replacement therapy for menopausal women is particularly worth mentioning. The patient who is taking this drug will be unwilling to stop because it suppresses the symptoms of her menopause and makes her feel physically young and fit. For any woman those are strong hooks and the 'addiction' can be a powerful one if the prescribing doctor is weak and not prepared to control the availability of this drug.

NON-PRESCRIPTION DRUGS

In Sweden, during the influenza epidemic of 1918, a doctor working at a big factory prescribed a powder which contained phenacetin for a large proportion of the workforce. The survivors of the flu epidemic felt that the powder had not only helped them to avoid the worst of the flu, but had also made them feel fitter and stronger. As a result they continued to take the powder, which was obtainable without a prescription, as a tonic.

It quickly became common practice in huge areas of Sweden to start the day with a phenacetin powder. People who visited friends in hospital would take them phenacetin powders instead of flowers or chocolates. The powders were even given as birthday presents. Thus, thousands of perfectly ordinary, sane people became addicted to a seemingly simple headache powder. It wasn't until evidence became available which showed that the powder was causing potentially fatal kidney damage that the habit was broken, and even then there was some resistance.

That is just one example of an over-the-counter medicine that produced thousands of addicts. There are many other drugs about which similar stories could be told.

These days the addictive over-the-counter drugs usually fall into a fairly small number of basic categories.

1. The vitamin and mineral products which people take as tonics. These drugs do not cause any physical addiction, but the people who take them invariably insist that without their drugs they will fall ill, get colds and feel weaker. All sorts of benefits have been claimed for vitamin and mineral mixtures and millions of people wouldn't dream of starting the day without their favourite product. The fact is, however, that taking vitamin supplements to get healthier or stay fitter is about as logical as trying to push another million volts into your television set so that you'll get a better picture. Since it is known that vitamin supplements have absolutely no useful function (unless the person taking them is following an inadequate diet), the only conclusion can be that the individuals concerned believe in the efficacy of the product so much that they are hooked. Tragically diseases *caused* by vitamin supplements are now probably more common than diseases caused by vitamin deficiencies.

2. The many different varieties of aspirin and mild pain-killer. During my years in general practice I met a number of patients who regularly took aspirin and who felt lost without it. They insisted that since aspirin tablets help cure headaches then daily aspirin tablets must also act as a preventative. They were hooked on hollow logic and over-the-counter aspirin tablets.

3. Cold cures and cough medicines. For example, the many different types of nasal decongestant on the market are addictive because they can produce the very symptoms that they are taken to relieve. The patient, unaware that his nasal congestion is being produced by the medicine that he is using, will continue with his own home treatment, perpetuating both his congestion and his need for the drug.

4. The laxatives. Enormous numbers of people throughout the 'civilised' world regularly use laxatives. They treat their bowels like naughty children or disobedient dogs and to punish them for not behaving properly swallow huge quantities of drugs. The problem is that many laxatives that are freely available without a prescription (including a number of so called 'herbal' products) have such a powerful effect that the bowel muscles get hooked. The result is that when the individual stops using his laxative he becomes constipated. Within a short time an apparently normal and healthy bowel can become totally dependent on pharmacological help. The owner of the bowel will have become a laxative addict.

5. Products containing caffeine. Most people get their caffeine from coffee or tea, cocoa or cola drinks, but there are also a large number of other products available over the chemist's counter which contain caffeine. Caffeine is a central nervous system stimulant which has a number of direct, physical effects. It pushes up the blood pressure and the heart rate, increases the amount of acid secreted in the stomach and produces clearer and faster thought processes. It is a powerful and potentially dangerous drug which can kill if taken in excessive quantities. It is also, without question, an extremely addictive drug and many millions of people are addicted to it in one or other of its many forms. (See page 94.)

EXERCISE

◙ SIGNS OF ADDICTION

The exercise junkie will probably exercise every day – whatever the weather. Even if feeling ill or 'out of sorts' he will take his exercise. He will probably get angry and upset if people criticise or question the type of exercise he favours. He will continue exercising even if he is in pain, whether or not it is caused by his activity, and will often try to persuade others to take up exercise.

◙ LONG TERM POSSIBLE EFFECTS

People who over-exercise risk injuring their bodies in many different ways. They damage joints, bones and muscles – and may have a heart attack if they push themselves too hard.

■ WITHDRAWAL EFFECTS

The exercise junkie who tries to cut down may feel physically uncomfortable as well as guilty, and may worry that he is missing out on 'beneficial' exercise.

■ GIVING UP

Exercise junkies need to be supported with friendship and reassurance as they cut down their exercise programme to a more sensible level. For example, family or friends may persuade them to take up swimming or join them in a brisk walk rather than jog compulsively. They may need to be taught how to relax and they will probably benefit from taking up less strenuous and demanding hobbies.

There are many types of exercise addict. There are those who do aerobic exercises, those who favour muscle building and weight lifting, those who specialise in field events and those who become hooked on sports as varied as cross-country skiing and cycling.

When people exercise for fun and enjoy what they do then I would not dream of describing that exercise as an addiction. We all need a hobby, and exercise of just about any kind is as good as any other interest. Indeed, for the individual who leads a largely sedentary life some regular exercise is essential for good physical health.

I believe that exercise becomes a problem, however, when people claim that it makes them immune to ill health, that it improves their sex lives and so on. Today, there are many individuals who exercise with almost religious fanaticism, dressing for the gym or the streets with the care and attention that others might prepare for church. These fanatics, who invariably berate non-believers with a passion common among zealots of all kinds, take pride in pushing themselves through the pain barrier and taking their bodies right to the edge. Like other addicts they will deny that they are addicted. But like other addicts they are damaging their bodies and they will need help if they are to 'kick' their addiction.

Consider jogging, for example.

I didn't realise that jogging or running could be addictive until I looked out of my window one terrible winter's day and watched a really miserable looking middle-aged man stumbling along the pavement. Now I've watched the antics of my neighbourhood joggers for some time, and have been constantly puzzled by their dedication. But this particular fellow defied all logical explanations. He was drenched, he was huffing and puffing, his face was contorted with pain and his feet were slapping on the wet pavement in a heavy, flat-footed, unathletic style. I couldn't convince myself that even he believed that what he was doing was improving his health.

All the available evidence suggests that even if you enjoy jogging, and do it in pleasant surroundings, it doesn't do you a great deal of good. Trotting along in freezing winter rain must be far worse for your health than sitting in front of the television with a glass of beer and a plateful of cheese and pickle sandwiches. So why was my jogger out there in the rain at all?

The only possible explanation I could produce was that he was addicted to what he was doing. And I think I can explain that addiction by relating it to the internal production of the endorphin hormones.

Endorphins

It has been known for some time that the human body is capable of producing its own internal, pain-relieving hormones which are as powerful as morphine, and, in their own way, just as addictive. It is the presence of endorphins in the human body which explains the 'placebo' response. When a doctor gives a sugar pill to a patient who is in pain, the patient gets better because his body is inspired to produce its own pain-relieving hormone.

As far as joggers are concerned (and this same argument applies to all exercise fanatics who push themselves through the pain barrier) the relevant evidence was disclosed by Jon D Levine, Newton C Gordon and Howard L Fields, of the Departments of Neurology, Physiology and Oral Surgery respectively at the University of California in San Francisco, in an article published in *The Lancet* in 1978.

These three authors did a good deal of vitally important work on endorphins and pointed out that the pain-relieving mechanisms through which morphine and placebos work seem to be similar. They pointed out that patients using placebos tend to use larger amounts as time goes by, and that when the placebo is withdrawn they often show signs of distress. With repeated use over long periods of time, the pain relief produced by placebos tend to become less effective.

All this suggests that it is possible to become addicted to placebos (and that means addicted to endorphins) in just the same way that it is possible to become addicted to morphine.

When a jogger or runner pushes himself through the pain barrier he is able to keep going because his body produces supplies of its own endorphins in an attempt to overcome the pain. The pain is produced as a warning sign. The jogger's body produces endorphins because it believes that it is not possible to stop and that the pain must be endured.

When this happens as an isolated instance, there are no problems. For example, if a soldier on a battlefield has an injured ankle but needs to keep moving in order to escape from the enemy, his body will produce endorphins to overcome the pain. The ankle injury may be made worse by the continued activity, but the soldier himself will have benefitted – he will still be alive – thanks to one quick blast of endorphins.

But joggers go out on the streets every day, and their bodies are constantly releasing supplies of endorphin in order to overcome the physical pain that running produces. That is where the problem arises. As the days go by the track-suited street hound needs larger and larger quantities of endorphin in order to fight back the pain. And since we know that endorphins are just as addictive as morphine, it is possible that the jogger will eventually get hooked on his own endorphins. In practice, that means that he has become addicted to jogging. Even when the weather is foul he has to go out, splashing through the winter slush, damaging his health and making himself miserable.

Cutting back

Whatever his particular passion may be, the exercise addict needs to be encouraged to temper his enthusiasm with common sense. He should be encouraged to ask himself exactly what he hopes to get out of his exercise addiction – he may then see how unrealistic his expectations are. He should be encouraged to put more time and effort into other less damaging, more sedentary hobbies and interests.

FOOD

■ SIGNS OF ADDICTION

The food addict will almost certainly be overweight unless

she is one of the compulsive over-eaters who deliberately make themselves vomit after eating, in which case she may well be slim or even emaciated. Food addicts, like other addicts, tend to be dishonest both with themselves and with others. They may keep a secret cache of their favourite food, lie about their eating habits and even steal money to pay for the food they need.

■ LONG TERM POSSIBLE EFFECTS

The food addict who becomes overweight will run the risk of developing all the problems associated with obesity. These include heart disease, diabetes and high blood pressure. The overweight individual is also more likely to suffer from disorders such as arthritis. The food addict who eats and then vomits in order to stay thin may suffer from problems produced by the repeated passing of powerful, burning acid through the oesophagus and mouth.

■ WITHDRAWAL EFFECTS

The food 'junkie' trying to kick her habit (food addiction is commoner among women than among men) will be nervous, edgy and irritable. She will fidget, probably be unable to keep still and be tearful or even depressed.

■ GIVING UP

The food addict who wants to give up over-eating will need comfort, support and help from those around her. She must be encouraged to eat only when genuinely hungry and to learn to stop eating when not genuinely hungry. She must be persuaded to reward herself with items other than food (magazines, clothes, flowers, etc) and to keep her fingers busy when watching television by knitting or sewing or even stroking a cat, rather than nibbling choco-lates, biscuits or nuts. She may benefit from joining a slimming organisation such as Slimmer Silhouette (see page 172).

As with other types of addiction it is important to find out why the addiction began. If circumstances and pressures are not altered the addict is likely to begin abusing food again soon after giving up.

For general advice on giving up and where to find help, see pages 165–172.

There are many types of food addiction and it is possible to get addicted to specific types of food for a variety of reasons – and with a variety of results.

The commonest and most damaging type of food addiction is probably the simple, straightforward urge to overeat. It is this simple urge that produces so much excess weight in our society and that can in turn be responsible for so much illness and unhappiness.

Parental conditioning

To a very large extent our eating habits are created by circumstances. If, when you were small, your parents rewarded your good behaviour and good deeds by giving you food then you will have grown up to associate particular types of food with praise and feeling happy. The reason why there are so many people who love eating sweet things is simply that these are the types of food that parents most commonly use as a reward. When a mother gives her child sweets because he has been 'good' or allows him to have his pudding only when he has eaten up all his vegetables she is training her child to associate food with behaviour and to learn bad eating habits.

Similarly, parents may instil a hatred of certain foods by forcing children to eat them. For example, if your parents made you eat cabbage even though you didn't like it and didn't want to eat it then you will almost certainly still hate cabbage and associate it with unhappiness and misery.

Incidentally, if your parents had given you spinach and cabbage as a reward and made you eat sweet things as a punishment you would now very probably love spinach and cabbage and hate eating anything sweet.

This type of food addiction is produced by a process known as conditioning and it can be very difficult to break. It is, indeed, this type of bad eating habit that is the cause of a great deal of obesity in the Western world. We all have an appetite control centre in our brains and if, from childhood, we are allowed to eat what we want, in the quantities we want, when we want to eat it then, by and large, we do not put on excess weight. Experiments done with children have shown conclusively that the appetite control centre is quite capable of deciding for us what foods we should eat and when we should eat them. Unfortunately, the parental conditioning that most of us go through destroys that natural ability and leads us to dietary confusion and distress.

Social pressures

This parental conditioning isn't the only force. We are also subject to other pressures. Women, in particular, are constantly under pressure to achieve the right shape and the right size. Dress designers, fashion writers and photographers are frequently telling women that they should be slender and boyish in looks. This type of pressure, when accompanied by other social and parental influences, can eventually result in the development of conditions such as anorexia nervosa and bulimia nervosa. These are not 'addictions', but they are disorders which are linked to our general attitude towards food.

Chocolate addiction

One of the foods most commonly used for comfort eating is chocolate. Advertisers have for years taught us to associate it with childhood and with happy times, but here there is another important factor involved apart from psychological conditioning.

There have been chocolate addicts for centuries but it was only fairly recently that researchers managed to show just why this particular foodstuff is likely to produce problems.

Dr David Schwartz, Dr Michael Liebowitz and Dr Donald Klein at the New York State Psychiatric Institute discovered that in the brain there is a naturally occurring substance called phenylethylamine, a substance that is structurally rather similar to the amphetamines. It is this naturally occurring chemical which is responsible for the highs and lows of being in love. If you are always falling in and out of love, and tend to get depressed when a love affair ends, the chances are that the amount of phenylethylamine in your brain fluctuates more than usual.

The reason why we feel particularly good when in love is that the amount of phenylethylamine in our brain is unusually high. The pleasure we feel is rather similar to that which an amphetamine user feels. When our love affair comes to an end, we experience the sort of low feeling that is common among amphetamine users when they stop using their drugs.

Chocolate is the only food which contains phenylethylamine in high quantities. It is hardly surprising, therefore, that it has become the standard Christmas and birthday present and the traditional gift for St Valentine's day. People get hooked on chocolate because it evens out the ups and downs of everyday life – and it is readily obtainable.

Caffeine addiction

Apart from chocolate the other exceptionally addictive food is caffeine – a powerful drug readily available in coffee, tea, cocoa and cola drinks. Caffeine is a central nervous system stimulant which has a number of direct, physical effects. It pushes up the blood pressure and the heart rate, increases the amount of acid secreted in the stomach and produces faster, clearer thought processes. It is a powerful and potentially dangerous drug that can kill if taken in excess. It is also an extremely addictive drug which millions of people take in one or other of its many forms. Anyone who feels uncomfortable without an early morning drink of tea or coffee or who develops headaches or other symptoms after an hour or two without a caffeine-rich drink is probably addicted to caffeine and would almost certainly benefit physically and mentally by cutting down or slowly withdrawing from the drug. Other symptoms of over-use include indigestion and palpitations.

Other food addictions

Addiction to both chocolate and caffeine can be genuine 'physical' addictions rather than 'psychological' addictions (as happens when people get conditioned to unhealthy eating habits). In the last few years scientists have shown that it is possible to get addicted to some other types of food – these include corn, wheat, milk, eggs and potatoes – in the same way that it is possible to get addicted to alcohol.

The nature of the problem produced will naturally depend upon the food concerned. If an individual is addicted to a calorie-rich food then he will quickly become overweight and will have great difficulty in losing that extra weight success-fully. When he tries to cut out the food which is causing the problem, the addict will suffer from withdrawal symptoms (such as headaches) which can be extremely unpleasant.

Anyone who finds that he eats one particular food in excessive quantities, and who feels uncomfortable when he has missed that food for a few hours, should regard addiction as a genuine possibility. When cutting out a foodstuff which has produced an addiction, the addict should be prepared to suffer unpleasant withdrawal effects for at least a week. The food should then be avoided for twelve months, after which it may be possible to reintroduce the addictive food back into the diet.

There are medical specialists dealing with food addiction, and anyone who believes that he or she could be a food addict should ask his or her general practitioner to arrange the appropriate referral.

GAMBLING

■ SIGNS OF ADDICTION

The addicted gambler will try to recoup his losses until he runs out of money. He will gamble on most days of the week and he will always spend his winnings on gambling. He will probably keep his gambling secret from family and friends for as long as possible, and will usually consider himself to be a skilful gambler. He will avoid people because of debts he has accumulated and will spend much of his day thinking about gambling. He will borrow or even steal money so that he can carry on with his habit and gambling will affect his home life and career. He may sell his own and his family's personal belongings in order to continue gambling.

■ LONG TERM POSSIBLE EFFECTS

Physical injury may occur when gambling debts remain unpaid and creditors prove to be violent. Gamblers may become irritable and bad-tempered when their losses mount up – wife and baby battering can then follow. Debts may lead a gambler to suicide. Anxiety and depression are common.

■ WITHDRAWAL EFFECTS

The true gambling addict will feel physically ill and unhappy when not gambling. He will be edgy and unable to settle.

■ GIVING UP

The gambling addict who wants to stop will have to stop completely. It is unlikely that he will be able to carry on gambling in a controlled way. While he is adjusting to his new situation, access to money should be restricted and wages or salary should be paid straight into a bank account held by a trusted relative or friend. This strategy will only work with the full co-operation of the addict, and will probably put severe pressure on the account holder – and on any relationship – at least, in the early stages.

Professional help from an accountant may be needed as the full extent of any debts accumulated will have to be examined, painful though this will undoubtedly be. The reforming gambler will need help from both his family and his doctor. He should try to develop new interests and adapt his daily routine so that he limits his exposure to gambling possibilities. He should keep away from clubs where there are gambling machines and from betting shops. He should not buy newspapers that carry extensive details of racing fixtures.

There are specialist organisations which will be able to help, Gamblers Anonymous being the most useful. The address is on page 172.

Addictive gambling may not be as common a problem as heavy drinking or smoking. And it may not cause such obvious, straightforward physical symptoms as addictions to drugs. But heavy gambling is far commoner than most of us realise. According to Dr R Hallet of the Addiction Research Unit at the Institute of Psychiatry in London, writing in the *Health Education Journal* in 1984, at least one third of the population of Britain gamble regularly and 80,000 are heavy gamblers risking far more than they can afford and dedicating their lives to gambling.

Gambling has become very much an everyday part of our society. Daily newspapers carry details of horse races, not because readers are necessarily interested in horse racing but because this is a major aspect of the gambling industry. Most popular daily newspapers run 'Bingo' competitions and even august journals such as *The Times* now run similar schemes. Sunday newspapers carry details of the football pools and you can bet on just about anything you like in a betting shop. There is hardly a sport or an activity in the world that has not been the subject of betting schemes. Bear-baiting and cockfighting became popular because they gave people an opportunity to gamble and possibly make money quickly. Today, greyhound racing, boxing and golf attract the punters with itchy palms.

Effects of gambling

Most people would probably claim that for them gambling is mild and harmless; a pleasant way to add a small thrill to days that could otherwise be dull and empty of hope. But then most people who drink alcohol are not addicted and would similarly claim that their pleasure is harmless enough.

The trouble is that gambling can be addictive and it can cause considerable social and economic distress. Moreover, in today's violent society, if you get into debt with the wrong people you may find yourself suffering physical damage if you fail to find the necessary money to keep them happy. The tragedy is that gamblers can continue to borrow money quite easily long after their credit should have run out. And it isn't just 'loan sharks' who hand out money. The large banks vie with one another for the right to give us money to spend. Our major financial institutions have not only helped to create our current inflationary climate but our large current gambling problem, too.

The addictive gambler is likely to lose his job, his home and his family. He is also quite likely to lose his health. Both men and women are involved. Traditionally it is men who bet on horses and dogs but these days many thousands of women are regularly spending their housekeeping in Bingo halls. Some go in search of excitement. Others start gambling because they are desperately short of money and see gambling as a solution.

Hallmark of a gambler

It is difficult to define an addictive gambler. But Gordon E Moody MBE, the honorary founder and patron of Gamblers Anonymous, tells the story of how when he was in Sydney, Australia, he heard of a man who had a dream night at the card table. He won everything and left the other

players broke. However, the gambler was so frustrated that
the action had ceased that he divided up his winnings among
his fellow gamblers so that they could all keep going.
That really seems to sum up the difference between the
individual who gambles because he wants the chance to win
some money and the one who is addicted to gambling as an
activity. The true addict is in love not with winning but with
gambling itself. He needs the thrill of the turning card or
spinning dice or Bingo caller's voice in just the same way as
the heroin addict needs his fix.

WORK

■ SIGNS OF ADDICTION

The workaholic finds it difficult to relax or take a holiday.
He will spend evenings and weekends working and will
worry constantly about work. He will have difficulty in
sleeping and may wake up at night to resume working on
current problems. He will not eat proper meals.

■ LONG TERM POSSIBLE EFFECTS

The workaholic's mental and physical health will suffer.
He will have an increased risk of developing a heart attack,
peptic ulceration, high blood pressure or other problems
known to be associated with heavy pressure and stress. He
will have an increased risk of developing depression or
some other serious mental problem.

■ WITHDRAWAL EFFECTS

The workaholic trying to reform will be edgy and restless
and will find it difficult to relax. Even if he can be physically still, he will have great difficulty in preventing his
thoughts from racing through new ideas for present and
future projects.

■ GIVING UP
Workaholics invariably have little self-esteem or confidence. They need to be given both by someone close to them who is prepared to encourage them to relax and rest more. They need constant reassurance and support. They need to be taught how to relax and encouraged to take up soothing and calming hobbies.

The word 'workaholic' is rarely taken seriously and, indeed, it may seem strange to describe 'work' as an addiction. However, the truth is that many people do get addicted to 'work' and this type of addiction can be extremely destructive.

The basic symptoms exhibited by the workaholic are fairly straightforward. He (and it is more often a 'he' than a 'she') gets to work very early in the morning and leaves last thing at night. He probably takes work home to study during what remains of the evenings and at weekends. He may find it difficult to delegate responsibility and will probably have few interests outside his work. Most of his friends will be colleagues and contacts and as his addiction develops he will have less and less time for 'trivial' family pursuits.

However successful he may be (and all that work very often means that he is extremely successful) the workaholic will still find it difficult to slow down or cut his work load.

What makes a workaholic
There are a number of reasons why people become workaholics.

One of the commonest is a sense of personal inferiority and inadequacy. A child who is constantly admonished by his parents for his failures at school or urged on to even greater success if he is bright, will grow up desperate to please and determined to succeed. Similarly, a child whose parents are sparing with their love and affection will grow up so anxious for their recognition and approval that he will dedicate his life to work.

An individual who has experienced a long period of poverty or unemployment may over-compensate for an unhappy period by constantly working hard. Even when he has a secure job and plenty of money in the bank he may still feel the need to keep pushing himself. He is likely to open secret bank accounts and deposit money in all sorts of places so that he can obtain some peace of mind.

Effects of being a workaholic

Workaholics, frequently 'over-achievers', are often extremely successful and much admired by others who do not see the pain associated with their success. For despite the material successes that a workaholic may enjoy, this sort of lifestyle can do a good deal of damage both to his own mental and physical health and to his relationships with those close to him. Despite their warnings and appeals the workaholic will keep pushing himself at the same cruel pace, regardless of his achievements and needs. He may have millions in the bank and homes all around the world but his insecurities and fears will be as strong as they were when he was just starting out. He will find it impossible to rest, relax or retire and will drive himself ever onwards, yearning for the praise and security that will probably never come. He will spend evenings and weekends working. He may wake up at night to resume working on current problems. He will have difficulty in sleeping. He will not eat proper meals.

Inevitably, all this will have an adverse effect on his health.

High blood pressure, heart disease and peptic ulceration are just three of the physical disorders which commonly afflict workaholics. Anxiety, depression and sleeplessness are common mental problems. Even when disease has been diagnosed the workaholic will probably find it difficult to slow down. And, sadly, as he pushes himself harder and harder so the drain on his physical and mental resources will make it ever more difficult for him to work effectively and efficiently. As his frailties make him less capable so his fears and uncertainties will gather force and he will find himself pushed to work still harder. When he tries to slow down he will be edgy and restless.

For the workaholic, life is a constant treadmill.

The only solution

Workaholics invariably have little self-esteem or confidence and need to be given both by someone close to them who is prepared to encourage them to relax and rest. They will need constant reassurance, approval and affection, and they will need to be encouraged to take up soothing and calming hobbies.

Without help of this sort the workaholic will probably work himself into an early grave. Sadly, many workaholics only recognise that they have a problem when a colleague with a similar affliction dies through overwork.

3

WHAT MAKES
AN ADDICT?

Personality
Pressure
Boredom
Advertising
Doctors

Cost
Fashion
Sex
Information

People become addicts for all sorts of reasons. On the pages which follow I describe some of the most important. One, some or all of these may apply to any one addict's personal circumstances. Only when it becomes clear why someone has become an addict will it be possible for him to help himself or be helped effectively. Read these sections carefully and look for pressures and signs that you recognise.

PERSONALITY

For many years experts around the world have argued about whether or not is is possible to define the type of individual most likely to become an addict. Such information would obviously be helpful since it would enable doctors to protect those patients most at risk.

For example, it has been suggested that the majority of addicts have personality problems which create social difficulties and that it is these social problems which are eventually responsible for their need to turn to drugs or other outside aids.

It has been argued that people who become addicts are invariably shy, sensitive and exceptionally nervous. They may produce a veneer of sophistication and strength but underneath that surface layer they are emotionally uncertain and in desperate need of love and affection. They have difficulty in forming close relationships with other people and find that drugs help them by providing them with relief, support or confidence. They are lonely and insecure and drugs give them comfort.

Other psychologists have argued that addicts are usually inadequate or inferior in some way and need drug support because they find themselves constantly failing to fulfil social expectations. They use as examples those addicts who have turned to drugs when they have been unable to satisfy their parents' ambitions. These people tend to be guilt ridden, hard working and vulnerable to criticism. They have little or no self-confidence and may well be far more successful than they realise. They are often driven by a deep sense of continuing despair and personal failure and may also feel an unexpressed, even subconscious, sense of anger towards one or both parents.

It has also been said that the majority of addicts are rather childish in their outlook, they tend to be depressives, their behaviour tends to be excessive, they are unusually intelligent and frustrated by their inability to make headway in life, they are disorganised, unruly, unable to cope with pressure and generally over-demanding.

All of the researchers seem to be suggesting that if there is one word that sums up the addict it is: immature. People take drugs because they cannot cope, and they cannot cope because they haven't become mature enough to deal with life's problems sensibly and dispassionately.

But I'm not sure that this takes us very much further forward. For the truth is that very few of us could ever claim to be totally in charge of our lives and always capable of coping with problems and pressures in a sensible way. Most of us would admit that under some circumstances we feel nervous or inadequate, incompetent or rebellious. Indeed, responses of that type can be an asset rather than a liability, an enriching factor rather than one likely to damage the quality of our lives. After all, it is uncertainty and insecurity which drive us onwards and upwards and it is vulnerability and rebelliousness which give us our creative faculties.

We will get absolutely nowhere by studying personality in isolation. And I would make two points to substantiate that claim.

First, the human personality is a fragile, vulnerable thing which we can do little or nothing to change and which should in any case be considered more or less inviolate. The individual can adapt his attitudes and expectations if they prove damaging or destructive. But he cannot change his fundamental personality, nor should he be encouraged to try. History is full of examples showing that those individuals with the weakest personalities have often made the most important contributions to society.

Second, it is not the personality of the individual which determines whether or not he becomes an addict but the circumstances in which he finds himself. We are all potentially vulnerable and we all have weaknesses and fears.

The only factor that separates the addict from the non-addict is that the addict has found himself in a situation where his personality has proved too fragile, while the non-addict has not yet strayed from an environment in which he is able to feel competent and in control. Anyone tempted to feel smug or self-satisfied at not being an addict should remember that it is often fate and fortune which determine our circumstances, our vulnerability and, eventually, our needs.

PRESSURE

On the face of it, 20th-century life doesn't look as though it ought to provide us with too much pressure. Those of us fortunate enough to be living in the Western world can usually get enough to eat and can almost invariably rely on having a roof over our heads. Generally, our basic needs are well satisfied. From the point of view of our ancestors, or indeed of the millions of less fortunate individuals living in less well developed parts of the world, we have few basic worries. Stone age man had to spend his days worrying about getting enough food and finding somewhere warm to sleep at night. We've got those fundamental problems well and truly cracked.

Yet there is little doubt that we now suffer far more from stress than our ancestors ever did. Moreover, evidence shows that although stress is the 20th-century equivalent of the plague, stress-induced disease being endemic in just about all the developed countries, it is relatively rare in underdeveloped or developing countries. And our extraordinary dependence on drugs is just one more consequence of our inability to cope with the stress which is such a factor in 20th-century life.

Basic cause of stress

There is one basic reason why we suffer so much from stress these days. And that is the fact that our bodies were designed a long, long time ago and are ill suited for modern society.

We were designed for the sort of instant world in which there is always likely to be a sabre-toothed tiger waiting just round the corner. And we were designed very well for circumstances like that. If we are faced with a sudden emergency our bodies respond quickly, dramatically and logically. Our muscles tighten, our hearts beat faster, our blood pressure goes up, adrenaline surges through our arteries, acid pours into our stomachs and our bodies are put on immediate alert. All these physiological changes are designed to help us survive the encounter. They help us fight, run, jump and climb with unusual and quite exceptional agility. The faster heart beat ensures that as much blood as possible reaches the muscles so that they receive a plentiful supply of oxygen. The rise in blood pressure has a similar purpose. The acid pouring into our stomachs ensures that any food that is there will be converted into usable energy, speedily and efficiently.

These basic traits were handed down from generation to generation for the very good reason that anyone who didn't respond in this instantaneous way wouldn't survive. Individuals who weren't able to run, jump, climb or fight well were eaten up by man-eating, marauding tigers. Individuals who did respond in an immediate way lived to produce and raise the next generation. Simple genetics have meant that through ordinary selection processes we are these days particularly well adapted for a world full of sabre-toothed tigers and immediate physical dangers.

Unfortunately, these natural, automatic responses are no longer appropriate. Indeed they are a hindrance rather than a help, for we have changed our world far more rapidly than our bodies have been able to evolve. Instead of being faced with a sabre-toothed tiger, a pack of hungry wolves or an angry boar we are far more likely to find ourselves having to face unemployment, large gas bills or officious policemen. None of these modern problems is easily solved. None can be dealt with by a faster heart beat, a higher blood pressure or tense muscles.

Never before in history have there been such dramatic changes. Attitudes, fashions, fears, feelings and ambitions have altered rapidly. Revolutionary changes in navigation, medicine, science, military tactics, agriculture, industry and so on have all changed the world a great deal. But our bodies are much the same as they were several thousand years ago. It takes thousands of years for the human body to adapt and we have moved far too quickly for our own good. Today our protective physical responses are sadly inappropriate.

When we find ourselves facing huge gas bills that we cannot pay, legal threats that we cannot cope with, unemployment caused by factors outside our control, officialdom that is backed by authority without being restricted by responsibility, or even the simple need to find a car parking space, we still respond in the old fashioned way. Our muscles become tense and our hearts beat faster. But responses designed for a physical threat are of absolutely no help in circumstances like that.

Indeed those traditional physical responses are doubly inappropriate, for our modern problems tend to continue for such long periods of time that an immediate physical response can become positively harmful rather than merely inappropriate. For example, if you are worried about inflation and possible unemployment, then your blood pressure will go up and your heart will beat faster for as long as your worries continue. That could well turn out to be months or even years.

One other important point that needs to be taken into consideration is that we all respond to stress in different ways. In practice it is not the pressure or the stress that causes the problems so much as the way that each individual responds. Someone with a high stress threshold may endure all sorts of hazards, threats and difficulties without suffering, while another individual, with a lower stress threshold, may suffer enormously when exposed to quite modest levels of stress and pressure.

The irony here is that the individual who is least likely to cope well with our modern world would be the one best able to cope with a world full of genuine physical threats. Those best suited to a world full of sabre-toothed tigers and other physical threats will suffer very quickly when faced with long term, insoluble problems. On the other hand, those whose responses to physical threats are slow, and who would therefore have had difficulty in a world full of physical problems, remain relatively unaffected by typical 20th-century problems and hazards.

Effects of stress

The consequences of all this stress and pressure vary too. Some individuals develop physical disorders, and there is a huge amount of evidence now available to link stress and pressure to such apparently straightforward physical problems as heart disease, asthma, stomach ulceration and skin disorders. Stress induced physical disease is extremely common these days and there seems little doubt that we are in the middle of a major epidemic of what is generally known as psychosomatic disease.

But though the physical problems caused by stress and pressure are commonplace, the mental problems produced seem to affect an even greater percentage of the population. Within every age group, every social group, every class and profession, every race and each sex, huge numbers of people suffer from one of the many common nervous disorders: anxiety, nervousness, sleeplessness and so on.

And it is nervous troubles that often lead to addiction of one sort or another.

The precise type of drug that a sufferer uses will depend very much on the nature of the environment in which the individual lives and on the type of people with whom he most commonly spends his time.

An international film star may turn to cocaine, a miner to beer or cigarettes and a housewife to one of the benzodiazepines. The type of drug chosen will also depend on local traditions and expectations. In the East the traditional way of dealing with pressure is to dampen down responses to stress. Opium and heroin are particularly well suited to that sort of requirement for both make the user feel calm, satisfied and contented. Drives, demands, expectations and ambitions are removed completely. In the West, however, people feel that they have to keep going and stay aggressive. And alcohol, which removes the inhibitions, is a much more suitable drug for that sort of response.

Finally, the type of drug an individual uses will also depend on the availability of medical care. Where there are doctors in plenty there will also be vast numbers of people using benzodiazepines.

BOREDOM

Boredom is one of the most under-rated pressures in our society. We tend to think of it as being nothing more than a mild, usually temporary nuisance. A fleeting irritation that can be cured with a good book, an interesting conversation or a pleasant walk in the country. The truth, however, is very different for there is now considerable evidence that boredom is a major cause of distress, anxiety and depression.

There are, I believe, five major groups of people particularly likely to suffer from boredom.

There are the millions who are unemployed and who see no prospects of finding employment. In just about every so-called civilised country a growing number of men and women know that they will probably never work again. And while that is bad enough, the horrors endured by young school leavers facing a lifetime of unemployment hardly bear thinking about. As factories become more automated and offices become more streamlined there is a smaller and smaller need for factory workers or office staff. And as the number of people gainfully employed in factories and offices falls, so the demand for service industries falls. For as long as we continue our love affair with computers and high technology we are trapped in this spiral and the levels of unemployment will continue to rise.

Because we live in a job orientated society where status and self-respect depend on having a job with some position and power, unemployment produces a number of very damaging forces. The individual who has lost a job, or who is unable to find a job at all, will undoubtedly feel a tremendous sense of guilt and failure. But there will also be seemingly endless days of dull, unremitting boredom.

Secondly, there are those whose jobs are undemanding, unrewarding and uninspiring. Not so many years ago, just about any job required skills of some kind. A craftsman would be expected to have agile fingers and skilful hands. A clerk would be expected to have a facility with words or figures.

Today, however, in offices and shops there are millions of employees whose jobs are quite free of responsibility. There are computers and word processors which can write letters, add up numbers, check spelling and keep files far more efficiently and rapidly than any clerk. In factories, there are countless thousands whose work demands nothing more than that they act as nursemaids to complex pieces of machinery which can turn out an endless series of perfect objects, created to standards that no craftsman could ever hope to match.

The machines have become the principals in just about all working relationships. And instead of doing work from which they can derive satisfaction and pride, men who might have once been regarded as skilled craftsmen simply babysit masses of machinery which deny their operators any opportunity for self expression, pride or pleasure.

Then there are the men and women who have voluntarily retired early. For several years now I have regularly read reports of trade union officials noisily campaigning for earlier retirement for their members. And yet when I was in general practice just a few years ago I watched a seemingly endless stream of men and women shuffle through my surgery, complaining that they had retired too soon. For even the simplest and least demanding of jobs still offers something in the way of authority, meaning, purpose, companionship and friendship. A man may complain about his job, his working conditions and his employer but at least he has something positive about which to complain. Even that simple pleasure, that fundamental human delight, is denied the individual who has retired too soon.

Fourthly, there are those children at school who can see no prospect for themselves other than years of collecting unemployment benefit. For them there can be no bright future, no dreams to harbour and no ambitions to nurture. Their school work becomes unbearably dull because they lose heart and see little point in struggling through academic chores that can lead them nowhere.

Finally, there are those housewives who, perhaps more

than any other group in our society, are modern day victims of boredom. They may live in comfortable homes in pleasant areas and be married to pleasant fellows with jobs that have pensions and fringe benefits. They may have a healthy, good-looking family, attractive, comfortable clothes, and all the trappings of a satisfying 20th-century existence. But their lives will probably be planned around pieces of household machinery: washing machines and tumble driers, freezers, microwave ovens and pop-up toasters. And their opportunities for self expression or real fulfilment will be slim indeed. The womens' liberation movement may have reminded them of their rights, but it has been able to do very little to help them achieve those rights.

I believe that for all these people boredom is a driving force that pushes them relentlessly along a road to one or other of the many forms of addiction, their choice naturally depending upon their circumstances. For example, the bored house-wife may end up taking tranquillisers. The bored school boy may start sniffing glue. Or if he lives in an area where heroin use is common he may become a heroin addict. And the man who is bored will probably turn increasingly to tobacco or alcohol for sustenance.

It has long been established that there is a link between unemployment and depression, between boredom and the search for risk and excitement provided by drugs. And in recent years it has been shown that the welfare state can be extremely unhealthy, for, as it takes away personal responsibility, so it produces a real need for thrills and excitement of some kind.

But boredom has remained consistently underestimated as a driving force. The reality of it all was perhaps best described by William Burroughs in his book *Junkie*. Describing his childhood, Burroughs wrote: 'At this time I was greatly impressed with the autobiography of a burglar, called *You can't win*. The author claimed to have spent a good part of his life in jail. It sounded good to me compared with the dullness of a Midwest suburb where all contact with life was shut out.'

'You become a narcotics addict,' wrote Burroughs, 'because you do not have strong motivations in any other direction. Junk wins by default. I tried it as a matter of curiosity. Most addicts I have talked to report a similar experience. They did not start using drugs for any reason they can remember. They just drifted along until they got hooked.'

With boredom behind their need for drugs it is hardly surprising that so many addicts return to drug taking within a year or two of giving up. It is often said that they return to their addiction because they cannot stand the uncomfortable symptoms of withdrawal. But when one understands the depths of boredom that are involved it is not difficult to conclude that many drug addicts take drugs not to ward off withdrawal symptoms but because the modest pleasures afforded by drug taking exceed the pleasures normally available to them.

ADVERTISING

The two major drug addictions that are affected by advertising are smoking and drinking; eating and gambling are influenced to a lesser extent. There is little doubt that advertising cigarettes and alcohol has a powerful effect on potential customers. Although most Western-style countries have some regulations governing the amount of advertising that can be done or the methods that can be used, the tobacco and alcohol companies have become extremely adept at making the best of the available facilities.

For example, although they are banned from advertising directly on British television, a number of tobacco companies get their brand names plenty of exposure on television by sponsoring sporting events. It seems as though every televised sport now has a cigarette company sponsoring some tournament or other.

And this type of advertising is effective. In a report

published in the *Health Education Journal* in 1984, Frank Ledwith, research fellow in the department of education at the University of Manchester, reported on a survey which involved 880 secondary school children in the city. Ledwith found that the children he questioned were most aware of those cigarette brands most frequently associated with sponsored sporting events on television. Indeed, by testing to see how many children recognised the name of a tobacco company before and after a sponsored snooker competition appeared on television, the research showed that sponsorship of a sport that is going to appear on television acts as very effective cigarette advertising.

There is one additional advantage in advertising products this way. People who watch the programmes and see the brand name on television quickly come to associate the name of the product with their sporting heroes. This gives the product glamour and status. In fact, it isn't difficult to argue that advertising a product by sponsoring a sporting event is probably better for a tobacco company than direct advertising could ever be. It is almost certainly true that by sponsoring a sporting event you can implant your product's name in the minds of young watchers (and they are the customers of the future) far more effectively than you could by buying straightforward advertising space.

Indeed, a growing number of advertising agencies are now aware that it often pays to plan promotional campaigns in unusual ways to attract customers to a product. One market research firm is said to have recommended to a large tobacco company that in order to sell its product to young people effectively it should forget about advocating low tar brands, and ignore the health question altogether. Instead, the company was advised to relate its advertising to adult activities such as sex and alcohol or link its products to illegal activities such as pot smoking. The market researchers recommended this aggressive approach because evidence suggests that you're more likely to persuade young children to start smoking by telling them that it's bad for them, and that it is illegal, than you are by pointing out that your brand has less tar than any other and is therefore much safer.

One of the big questions about tobacco and alcohol advertising concerns the effectiveness of the advertising in attracting new recruits. Both the tobacco industry and the alcohol industry seem to argue that their advertising is purely designed to persuade existing smokers and drinkers to switch brands, rather than to encourage non-smokers or non-drinkers to start drinking or smoking.

Indeed in a publication called *The Impact of Advertising on the United Kingdom Alcoholic Drink Market*, published in 1983 by the Advertising Association, Dr L W Hagan and M J Waterson claimed that 'alcohol advertising is virtually entirely specific brand orientated advertising: it is promoting a particular name of beer or spirits, etc; it is never promoting alcoholic drink as a total concept.' The authors also claim that: 'only a very small fraction of the population can be classed as alcoholics or as abusing alcohol in a serious manner.' The independence and authority of the Advertising Association can perhaps be judged from that rather remarkable statement.

Personally, I don't think that this argument stands up very well to examination. Apart from the fact that tobacco companies continue to advertise even when they have a monopoly, it is extremely difficult to accept that advertising which shows a man enjoying a successful or pleasant lifestyle while also smoking a cigarette will have no effect on young, uncommitted viewers.

Although there is no evidence to prove my contention, I firmly believe that the advertising of tobacco and of alcohol has had a most powerful effect on the number of people using those two drugs. And as supporting evidence I would point to the developing countries around the world where the tobacco companies and alcohol companies are now selling their products in ever increasing quantities, and where death rates from diseases caused by tobacco and alcohol are rocketing.

There seems little doubt that the tobacco and alcohol industries are now anxious to improve their sales in developing countries so that their profits can be maintained should campaigns against alcohol and tobacco be successful in the West. To encourage new smokers and drinkers the advertising companies are using cynical and aggressive advertising tricks that would be banned in more civilised parts of the world.

We should undoubtedly seek out and arrest the men who trade in such drugs as heroin and cocaine, but we should reserve our greatest contempt for those elegant, well educated executives who work for the tobacco industry, the alcohol industry and the advertising industry. These men, with their children at preparatory schools, their country homes, cocktail parties and smart motor cars, are well aware of what they are doing. These are truly men who represent the 'unacceptable face of capitalism'.

DOCTORS

One of the major factors in the rising incidence of drug addiction in recent years has been the role played by the medical profession. And one of the true ironies of the 20th century is the fact that a huge speciality within the profession has been formed to deal with problems largely created by doctors themselves. A small part of the problem has been caused by the deliberate and callous provision of drugs for money, but the greater part of the problem results from carelessness and simple ignorance. Doctors have also contributed to the addiction problem by playing a significant part in the development of a society in which pills and drugs of all kinds are over-valued.

The precise size of the part played by doctors in our modern drug addiction problem is impossible to estimate. Too many other factors are involved. But the significance of the medical contribution is well illustrated by the way that the heroin problem developed in Britain in the 1960s.

At that time there were relatively few heroin addicts in Britain – no more than a few score – and no one took the problem very seriously. The British medical establishment (those doctors who speak for the profession in public) certainly didn't think that the problem merited special precautions.

Although steps had been taken in other countries to control the supply of heroin through specialist centres, British doctors insisted on retaining their prescribing freedom. It was argued that if doctors simply gave the addicts they saw the precise amount of heroin that they needed then the problem could be controlled without too much difficulty. The main advantage of this system was seen as the fact that it would keep black marketeers out of the country. If heroin addicts could get their supplies without any difficulty there would be no incentive for smugglers to move into the country. (In fact, the number of addicts was so small that there was no incentive for drug smuggling anyway.)

The main snag with the system was that it relied on doctors prescribing the right quantities for the addicts that they saw. And that was where the system broke down.

The relatively small number of doctors who were prepared to have anything to do with Britain's heroin addicts weren't capable of making such close judgments accurately. Either through greed or carelessness, or through straightforward gullibility, the doctors who were prescribing for heroin addicts overprescribed. They didn't have the time or the skills to develop bonds with their patients and simply ended up handing out prescriptions.

There were never more than about half a dozen doctors prescribing for Britain's addicts. Working mainly in and around Harley Street these doctors helped to found Britain's heroin problem by prescribing in such huge quantities that their patients were able to sell their excess supplies. Within a remarkably short time the number of heroin addicts in London had multiplied many times. And by the time the authorities stepped in and stopped doctors prescribing heroin freely the situation was perfectly poised for the black marketeers to move in. When the Brain Committee on Drug Abuse, which was eventually responsible for the introduction of the *Misuse of Drugs Act* in 1971, reported, it announced that of the 46Kg of heroin used for medical treatment in one year in the 1960s, some 42Kg had been prescribed by just six doctors! Heroin prescribing has largely been done by doctors practising privately, but not all the prescribing has been done purely for money. Many of the doctors involved undoubtedly believed that they were helping addicts by supplying them with drugs; others were 'frightened' into providing prescriptions.

Problem has spread

The overprescribing of heroin in the 1960s was particularly reprehensible but there have been other similar problems since then which have highlighted the weakness. Indeed, the problem has spread nationwide. In the 1960s the doctors who were overprescribing nearly all worked in central London (most of them had consulting rooms in Harley Street). Today, although there are still doctors in central London who overprescribe, the problem has spread to the provinces and in most cities of Britain it is possible to find one or two doctors who are dishing out dangerous pills quite freely. From time to time national newspapers print stories about these doctors, frequently including their names and addresses. The stories that are published rarely do any good but usually make it clear to addicts where they can obtain supplies at the best possible rate.

In 1982, a doctor said to have written up to 10,000 private prescriptions a year and to have charged an average of £10 for every prescription was suspended from practice. The General Medical Council was told that three of his patients had died after injecting themselves with a solution made from a synthetic opiate. That particular doctor was no back street peddlar. He was a member of his Area Health Authority, a vice chairman of a Local Social Services Committee, a chairman of the Boards of Governors of two local schools and a local councillor.

Not that the General Medical Council always strikes off doctors who prescribe with undue enthusiasm. In November

1984 it was reported that heroin addicts had been flocking to a doctor's surgery in Birmingham because he was known as a soft touch for drugs. He was reported to have handed out prescriptions for drugs for a £7 consultation fee. That particular doctor wasn't even struck off the medical register. He was banned from general practice but allowed to continue working in hospitals.

With this sort of thing going on all the time it is hardly surprising that in December 1982, H B Spear, Chief Inspector, Home Office Drugs Branch in London, wrote that the 'overspill from doctors' prescribing has for many years been a major element in the UK illicit market in controlled drugs.'

Allied problems

While the overt overprescribing of drugs has had a dramatic influence on the size of Britain's heroin problem, the overprescribing of other drugs, particularly tranquillisers and sleeping tablets, has created other worries such as the barbiturate and benzodiazepine crises. With these drugs the major factor behind the development of the problem has been that doctors have continually sought a medical solution to a series of social disorders. Traditionally, doctors are trained to think in simple, straightforward terms. They see all disorders starting as a result of biological, chemical or electrical abnormalities and they see the solutions as consisting of drugs.

The tragedy is that many of the symptoms that patients take into the doctor's surgery these days are caused by social problems for which there can be no pharmaceutical answer. And although doctors will tell a drinker that it is dangerous to take alcohol in an attempt to relieve real life problems (for that is often how alcoholism starts), they prescribe drugs such as barbiturates and benzodiazepines for patients with physical or mental symptoms caused by social problems for which, similarly, there is no pharmacological solution.

If a drug works at all, addiction is then inevitable, for the patient will learn that as soon as he stops taking the drug his original symptoms will recur.

Any drug that is given to treat anxiety must, if it works, be addictive.

The additional cruel irony is that the drug the patient is taking will make it less likely that he will be able ever to solve his own problems. By numbing the individual's mind and slowing down his thought processes (which is what all anti-anxiety drugs do), the doctor damages the patient's ability to deal with his real problems. And so the trap is tightened and complete. The patient's circle of addiction is turned into a restrictive noose from which there is often no escape.

Most of us will buy a friend a drink if we know he's nervous and anxious. In our hearts we know it's probably not the sensible thing to do, but we do it out of compassion. That is exactly what has been happening in doctors' surgeries for decades. Except that instead of buying their patients a single evening of blissful forgetfulness, doctors are prescribing blissful forgetfulness by the month.

What is perhaps most surprising about the fact that doctors continue to prescribe drugs for the treatment of anxiety is that they persist in the belief that one day there will be a drug available that will work without producing addiction. That suggests an ignorance about the human spirit which must worry us all. For it is not the drug alone that produces the addiction: it is a combination of the drug, the individual's needs and his circumstances. And of those three the nature of the drug is perhaps of least significance.

Doctors have to remember that it is impossible to produce any effective relief from anxiety and not run the risk of producing an addiction to the agent responsible for providing the relief.

The other tragedy of this modern medical affection for anxiolytic drugs is that it has spread to the patients. These days there are huge numbers of men and women who honestly believe that there is never any need to suffer from fear, anxiety, worry or even unhappiness. Through countless magazine and newspaper articles men and women have been encouraged to believe that drug therapy for unacceptable mood changes is efficient, effective and available.

As a result, doctors are besieged by patients expecting miracle solutions. There are no solutions, of course, and so doctors continually prescribe the only treatment available to them: anxiolytic drugs in greater and greater quantities. And they have created for themselves the biggest drug addiction problem in the history of the world.

These days there is a high level of acceptance for all prescribed drugs. Despite the recent scares and fears most people are still quite certain that prescribed drugs are safe. Many would probably argue that anything prescribed by a doctor isn't really a 'drug' at all.

Indeed, the demand for drugs has grown so rapidly in the last decade or so that doctors have had to introduce more 'efficient' schemes for handing out prescriptions. For example, many now provide anxiolytic drugs and sleeping tablets on repeat prescriptions. This means that patients can get a supply of tablets without going anywhere near the surgery or doctor. A telephone call or a letter to the receptionist results in a prescription being left out for collection or at least sent by return mail. The repeat prescribing of modern drugs is one of the major reasons why there are so many addicts today.

What really frightens me about the role of the medical profession in modern drug addiction is that it seems to be increasing rather than getting smaller. Despite an enormous amount of evidence to show that new drugs described as non-addictive very often turn out to be addictive, many doctors seem invariably enthusiastic about new products, accepting the manufacturers' claims with remarkably little cynicism.

The only possible explanation for this is that doctors are addicted to prescribing just as much as patients are addicted to swallowing.

And they are addicted to prescribing for one very important reason: they don't know what else to do.

Trained to prescribe
These days doctors spend much of their surgery time struggling to deal with problems for which they have never had

any training. Most were trained to deal with physical disorders and physical symptoms. Today most of their patients have psychological problems and mental symptoms. The traditional medical answer to a physical problem is to prescribe a drug. Just a hundred or so years ago, doctors didn't get paid anything *unless* they handed over a drug. There are no appropriate solutions for modern psychological problems and for the physical symptoms caused by stress and pressure. But doctors prescribe a drug because they have nothing else to offer.

It is because of this need to prescribe that doctors have become so anxious to protect their right to prescribe at all costs. Without a prescription pad a doctor is emasculated. It is this fear that leads doctors to protest vociferously when anyone wants to curtail their prescribing freedom or encroach upon it. And this fear will undoubtedly lead to still more drug addictions in years to come. Voluntary organisations and other members of the healing professions will be left with the task of trying to solve these problems as best they can.

The best hope for the future is that patients will be more and more reluctant to seek pharmacological answers to social and mental problems, less willing to accept prescriptions for drugs, more enthusiastic about sorting out their problems themselves and learning to take full advantage of the human body's astonishing self-healing powers, and more imaginative about accepting non-drug solutions.

COST

Obviously, the price of a drug has a tremendous influence on the number of people taking it. It is no coincidence that when schoolchildren first started taking heroin in huge numbers, in 1984, the price of the drug had fallen to an all-time low. Nor is it a coincidence that the drug most commonly used by young children – glue – is also one of the cheapest psychoactive products available.

What is more surprising is the fact that governments have

rarely used price as a serious restricting factor on the sale of addictive drugs.

For example, in a report published in October 1984 which suggested that heavy drinking costs Britain over a billion pounds a year in illness, accidents, crime and loss of working hours, it was pointed out that during recent years the real cost of alcohol has steadily declined. Indeed, today it takes roughly half as long to earn the price of a pint of beer as it did 30 years ago – and that despite the fact that the tax on beer has gone up much more sharply than the tax on spirits.

There seems little doubt that a modest increase in the price of alcohol would result in a fall in the amount of alcohol consumed. A study done by a team of Edinburgh researchers, who recently interviewed a representative sample of 500 members of the public, showed that the single most frequently cited reason for cutting down on alcohol consumption was the price. Even heavy drinkers said that they always cut down when the price went up.

This conclusion is supported by the fact that in 1981–2 the *per capita* British consumption of alcohol fell as a result of a modest increase in the tax on alcoholic drinks. That tax increase, however, was *not* as a result of any determined Government policy. It was but an accidental consequence of the economic recession which caused the Treasury to search for a quick money supply.

I have little doubt that it is the Government's reluctance to raise taxes on alcohol and tobacco that has resulted in the increased number of problems caused by these two substances. One must assume that pressure from the industries concerned, allied with the Government's natural fear of disappointing or annoying the electorate, has outweighed its determination to preserve the state of the public health.

FASHION

There are fashions in drugs just as there are fashions in clothes and motor cars. One of the major drug fashions in the

United States of America at the moment concerns cocaine. The use of this drug was almost unknown a few years ago but in 1983 a report in *Time* magazine showed that 11 percent of American adults now admit to having tried the drug on one or more occasions. The American cocaine industry is about three times as big as the recording and movie industries put together, involving some 45 tons of cocaine a year and bringing in something in the region of $25 billion annually. The fashion for using cocaine has become so strong among young professionals that the laws regulating its use are regarded by many as being as out of date as the prohibition laws were in the earlier part of the century. Among some young business people, using cocaine has become as fashionable as the two martini lunch once was.

Across the border in Mexico, on the other hand, one of the most fashionable drug abuses involves the inhalation of volatile products. Groups of young children who have left home roam the streets and get their kicks from cheap but potentially lethal substances such as glue. This type of addiction has become a major problem in Mexico.

While cocaine is fashionable among rising American businessmen and celebrities of all kinds, and glue sniffing is common among children in Mexico, the fashion among middle-aged women throughout the Western world is for tranquillisers such as those in the benzodiazepine group. Women now take drugs like Valium for the same reason that women living in the slums of Manchester took opium in the 19th century: because for them it is the one widely available, generally acceptable drug to have a useful effect on the mind. Generally speaking the benzodiazepines are, like marijuana, a middle-class drug. Cocaine is an upper-class drug. Heroin is a lower-class drug. There are, of course, exceptions to these general rules.

These fashions in drug taking have a powerful influence on the types of drug that are most widely used. In some areas of the world an individual who wants to become acceptable socially, or wants the approval of his peers, must become a regular drug user. Among some traditional West Indian groups it is more acceptable to use marijuana than not to use it. Among the hillside villagers of remote parts of the Andes it is still more usual to chew coca leaves than not to chew them. Among working men in the North of England a teetotaller stands out like a streetwalker in a nunnery – and for different reasons will probably feel as uncomfortable.

The 14-year-old who thinks that all his school friends are using heroin will, tragically, feel left out of things if he doesn't use heroin too. The slightly shy young man whose friends all smoke tobacco may feel embarrassed if he doesn't start smoking too. The college student whose colleagues all smoke marijuana may feel a social need to join in and smoke marijuana.

Even more significant, however, is the way that the general fashion for using drugs of all kinds has pervaded our society at just about all levels. Children grow up regarding drugs as a normal part of everyday life. They see their parents using drugs to avoid conception, to get to sleep and to treat mild headaches.

It is hardly surprising that they also accept that drugs can be used to help eradicate boredom, to help deal with pressure or to cope with a heavy work load.

The widespread nature of drug abuse in the 20th century must, to a certain extent, be blamed on those members of the medical profession and the drug industry who have so successfully persuaded us to regard drug use as an essential part of life in the 20th century. It is a cliché to say that 'familiarity breeds contempt' but it is certainly true about drugs. We have learned to use drugs and to take advantage of their powers. We have not yet learned to fear them.

SEX

I doubt if there is any addictive drug in the world that has not at some stage in its career been regarded as an aphrodisiac. And there are undoubtedly many present-day addicts whose initial courtship with drugs was inspired by thoughts of sexual success, or perhaps unusual or exceptional levels of pleasure.

Alcohol is an excellent example of a drug that is frequently used for its qualities as an aphrodisiac. And it is perfectly true that since alcohol can help release inhibitions it can release desires that would otherwise remain hidden and increase the chance of intercourse taking place. Many people (both men and women) have suppressed sexual feelings and alcohol tends to remove those restrictive inhibitions. The snag is that whereas a relatively small quantity of alcohol does act as an aphrodisiac, a larger quantity is quite likely to make a man impotent and a woman incapable of having an orgasm.

Marijuana is another drug with a powerful reputation as an aphrodisiac. Next to alcohol, marijuana is probably the most commonly used recreational drug in the world, but what effect it has on sexual activity has not yet been defined – although research work has been done on the subject.

When Dr Erich Goode of the State University of New York asked 200 marijuana users to explain how the drug affected them, nearly three quarters of the sample claimed that marijuana enhanced their sexual response. They said that marijuana could improve the quality of a sexual experience but could not increase their desire for someone they did not find attractive. Regular marijuana users also claimed that they had better orgasms after using the drug.

Some observers, I should add, have argued that people who use marijuana enjoy better sex because they feel that the drug frees them from normal restraints; it acts as an excuse for behaviour about which they would normally feel guilty or ashamed.

In America, the drugs traditionally regarded as having aphrodisiac qualities have been coca, peyote and psilocybe mexicana (also known as the magic mushroom). Coca, currently fashionable when used as cocaine, was popular some 3,000 years ago as a 'party' drug among members of the Inca royal family. Peyote is a cactus plant found just south of the

Rio Grande in Mexico, and it is from this plant that the hallucinogenic drug mescaline is obtained. Oddly enough, although mescaline has been used for hundreds if not thousands of years, it was only in the 1960s that the drug first acquired a reputation as an aphrodisiac. Of these drugs the one most vigorously claimed to be a 'sex drug' is the hallucinogenic mushroom psilocybe. Back in the 17th century a Spanish priest alleged that people who ate the mushroom would be 'provoked to lust'. Don Juan used the mushroom, too, and in the last couple of hundred years there have been numerous instances when the drug's qualities as an aphrodisiac have been reported.

The truth is that none of these substances has any real effect as an aphrodisiac. You can't turn someone on just by giving them one of these drugs; the best you can hope for is that normal inhibitions will be reduced or sensations of pleasure will be enhanced.

Still, those properties alone are enough to encourage many users and there is little doubt that however much they may have been exaggerated, the powerful reputations of these products have attracted many men and women over the last few decades. These days the drug most commonly described as having a powerful sexual effect is cocaine, and many regular cocaine users started the habit in the hope of enjoying better sex lives.

And, after all, it really doesn't matter whether or not a particular drug does have a powerful sexual effect or not. The placebo response is just as likely to work with an aphrodisiac as with any other drug – that is, the man or woman who *believes* that one of these drugs will make him or her feel sexier, or enjoy sex more, will undoubtedly benefit.

The danger is that having taken the drug and enjoyed better sex, the drug user will come to rely on the product. It is possible to get hooked on a drug even when you only *think* it is working. Indeed, that is the basis of many types of addiction.

INFORMATION

I believe that many people who ought to know better unwittingly encourage drug users and help to perpetuate myths and misunderstandings about potentially dangerous products.

For example, on 25th October 1984, the *Daily Telegraph* reported that Judge Richard Pearce QC, sitting in the Inner London Crown Court, had defended the use of the drug LSD so long as it was taken by 'happy, well-adjusted undergraduates sitting round a fire listening to nice music.' The hazards of LSD have been overemphasised in the past. But they haven't been overemphasised that much.

In December 1984 a leaflet produced by the Hereford and Worcester County Council for use by its social workers was reported in the *Daily Mirror* of December 7, as including the comment: 'do not be afraid to point out that some familiar glues, already commonly used, are relatively safe if used sensibly.'

In August 1985, the *Mail on Sunday* reported that in a medical training manual for doctors, sponsored by the Beecham drug company, Dr John Fry claimed that although adolescent solvent abuse is undesirable, it 'may be better than smoking or alcohol if they must do something.'

With drug users getting such advice from people in positions of responsibility it is hardly surprising that the number of drug users in Britain has never been higher.

CHAPTER

4

SOLUTIONS

The Legislative Approach
The Medical Approach
The Unofficial Approach

This chapter deals in detail with some of the ways in which doctors, lawyers, politicians and voluntary workers have tried to help individual addicts, and tried to deal with the addiction problem in general.

THE LEGISLATIVE APPROACH

Men and women have been using drugs to help them escape from the painful aspects of real life for centuries. A quick look through the history books will confirm that substances such as opium, cannabis, coca leaves and alcohol have been used more widely and more consistently than any purely medicinal drugs. During the last century or so, however, the problems associated with drug use have been intensified by the fact that scientists have not only been able to introduce more potent forms of these traditional products, but have also provided synthetic drugs.

In addition, the whole nature of drug use has been altered by basic changes in our society. For example, international travel has broken down all national barriers. A century or two ago each country had its own home-grown drugs, and local customs and traditions invariably controlled the way that any drug was used. Today you can buy just about any drug in almost any country in the world. And traditional methods of use have long since been overwhelmed and forgotten. The creation of a world market has also meant that drugs of all kinds have become the subject of massive international trade. Those drugs which Western countries regard as legally acceptable are distributed by legally organised corporations. The drugs which Western countries don't regard as legally acceptable are distributed by illegal, but equally well structured, organisations.

All this has meant that there has been a dramatic increase in the size of the drug addiction problem during the last century or so. Inevitably, this in turn has resulted in numerous attempts being made to control the distribution and use of drugs which have an effect on the mind. Governments don't like their citizens using drugs for the very simple but important reason that when people are bombed out of their minds they don't work very well. And while the bills for health care go up, industrial profits go down. So, during the 20th century governments around the world have united in an attempt to introduce controlling legislation and deal with drug abuse.

First international controls

The first international body to be concerned with the control of narcotic drugs was the International Opium Commission which met in Shanghai in 1909 and consisted of representatives from 13 countries. Their deliberations led to the signing (at the Hague) of the first drug control treaty: the *International Opium Convention* of 1912 which, for the first time, established international co-operation in the control of narcotic drugs as a matter of law.

Unfortunately, it takes time to get international treaties

signed and ratified and when the First World War broke out in 1914 only six countries had signed the Convention. And despite the fact that after the First World War, the signed peace treaty included signature of the Hague Convention, drug use around the world continued to increase well into the 1920s.

During the early post-war years the League of Nations created its own Opium Advisory Committee and at a convention held in Geneva in 1925, under the auspices of the League of Nations, another piece of international legislation was introduced.

This included a number of changes which made it more practical, more positive and potentially more powerful than previous attempts to control the use of opium. But the most significant aspect of the 1925 Convention was that it included cannabis as well as opium. Indeed, the legislation went so far as to include cannabis as a dangerous, narcotic drug. As I've already explained (see page 39) cannabis was included in the Convention to satisfy Egypt, and there was little or no evidence to support the suggestion that cannabis was a dangerous drug. However, the impact of this decision has had a powerful effect on all subsequent drug legislation, on the effectiveness of drug control campaigns and on the attitudes of drug users. In retrospect, the association of cannabis with opium undoubtedly weakened the effectiveness of what might otherwise have proved to be useful and restrictive legislation.

Since the 1925 Convention was signed, a number of other conferences have been held and other treaties and conventions have been signed. In 1931 a convention was signed which aimed to limit the manufacture and distribution of narcotic drugs, in order to meet the needs of the medical and scientific communities. In 1936, a fourth international convention was held to make illicit drug trafficking a crime internationally.

Post-war changes
The Second World War undid much of the good done by the

conventions held in the 1920s and 1930s but, since then, the United Nations and the World Health Organization have taken over the international control of drugs with most of the functions exercised by the League of Nations being transferred to the United Nations. Since the late 1940s a number of changes have been made on a practical level. For example, whereas in pre-war years the products under control were related to just three plants: the opium poppy, coca bush and cannabis plant, the 1948 legislation brought a number of synthetic substances under direct control. In 1971, a convention on psychotropic substances extended the international drug control system to cover hallucinogens such as LSD, sedatives and hypnotics such as the barbiturates and stimulants such as the amphetamines. A number of international treaties have been signed to ensure that controlled substances are used exclusively for medical and scientific purposes and to help individual governments prevent drug abuse.

Drug control organisations

Today, the United Nations has a number of drug control organisations under its wing.

1. The Economic and Social Council is responsible for formulating United Nations policy, co-ordinating drug control activities, supervising the implementation of international conventions and making recommendations to individual governments.

2. The Commission on Narcotic Drugs assists by considering what changes may be required in the existing machinery so that narcotic drugs and psychotropic substances can be controlled effectively on an international basis.

3. The International Narcotics Control Board is responsible for helping governments to limit the cultivation, production and use of drugs controlled by international conventions to the amounts needed for medical and scientific reasons. One of the ways in which to do this, is by producing a series of statistical aids to help governments estimate how much of each drug will be needed.

The Secretary General of the United Nations is himself assisted directly by a Division of Narcotic Drugs, and there is also a United Nations fund for Drug Abuse Control which is intended to provide resources for the control of drugs in parts of the world where funds are too restricted for the country concerned to take on such a responsibility itself.

Of the organisations which are in existence, however, few have done more for drug control than the World Health Organization which, on a number of occasions, has investigated areas of drug abuse and published vitally useful information. However, even the World Health Organization has found it difficult to make much progress simply because it is rarely possible to persuade scores of different governments to follow a single policy. For example, the World Health Organization's brave and sensible suggestion that the manufacture of heroin should be banned completely (on the grounds that the drug is not essential and that banning it completely would reduce the quantity being manufactured and greatly simplify controls) was squashed by Britain's refusal to accept this proposal.

The thinking behind all these treaties and conventions and of all the concomitant legislation that has been introduced in countries around the world (both as a result of conventions introduced by the United Nations and League of Nations and as a result of independent political pressure or legislative needs) has been that it is both wise and practicable to attempt to control drug abuse by legislation.

Ineffectual legislation

In practice, experience suggests that laws don't necessarily stop people dealing in drugs or using them and that, on the contrary, attempts to legislate against drug use may have made things worse rather than better.

As a quick example of a way in which apparently sensible and logical legislation can backfire with disastrous results one has to look no further than the American attempts to control alcohol.

Back in December 1917, after a considerable amount of

pressure from organisations such as the Women's Christian Temperance Union, the American Senate passed the 18th Amendment; an addition to the American constitution designed to prohibit the production, transport or sale of alcohol. The precise rules of prohibition were defined in the Volstead Act of 1919.

Prohibition was one of the most extraordinarily unsuccessful attempts at drug control ever introduced. Despite the fact that the American Government introduced thousands of prohibition agents to ensure that no one made, sold or used alcohol, criminals took advantage of public demand and ensured that alcohol could still be obtained quite readily. In the mid 1920s, in New York alone, there were said to be more than 30,000 speakeasies where alcohol could be bought. Al Capone is believed to have controlled over 10,000 speakeasies in Chicago.

By 1933 it was clear that prohibition wasn't working because public opinion was so united against it that the Government was never likely to achieve any sort of compliance with its laws. So the 21st Amendment to the United States constitution was passed, the prohibition laws were repealed and the legal sale of alcohol was allowed once more.

But the damage had been done and by 1933 America had acquired a massive underground network of well-organised criminals. Prohibition had given men like Al Capone the opportunity to build up an empire and to make huge amounts of money. Within the 15 years or so that prohibition lasted in America a whole generation of crooks had succeeded in creating for themselves a nation-wide industry.

When the prohibition laws were repealed, criminals needed other products to sell in order to maintain their organisations and their lavish lifestyles. As a result many started importing and selling drugs such as heroin. Through well-intended legislation, America had created a criminal force it could not control.

A common problem with legislation is that it frequently seems quite arbitrary when looked at dispassionately, because it is usually a compromise produced by a number of different pressures. The British refused to let China ban opium in the 1830s (even though the Chinese were worried about the problems associated with the drug) because it was in Britain's commercial interest to maintain opium sales. Britain actually fought a war in 1842 to protect its rights to sell opium. A few decades later Britain fought to have opium banned.

One of the most arbitrary and contentious pieces of legislation was the inclusion of cannabis in the international convention signed at Geneva in 1925, under the auspices of the League of Nations. The inclusion of cannabis had a number of unforseen and unfortunate effects. Apart from the fact that to control the use of cannabis individual countries have to spend huge amounts of money that would be better directed into the control of more dangerous products, as a result of this association between opium products and cannabis many people around the world do not regard opium (usually now available as heroin) as a serious problem. They know that cannabis is not a dangerous drug and so assume that the risks associated with opium have been exaggerated. The arbitrary upgrading of cannabis has had a counterproductive effect and has resulted in many drug users ignoring warnings about opium and its derivatives.

These days the whole problem is exacerbated by the fact that laws around the world still vary considerably and that drugs which are unacceptable in one country will be socially acceptable and perfectly legal in another country. For example, alcohol is banned in some Middle Eastern countries but is accepted as a natural social aid in most Western countries. These variations in customs and legislation make life much easier for smugglers and drug dealers; it also becomes difficult for a drug user to take any legislative control seriously.

Another reason for being wary about introducing drug control legislation is that many drug users are actually attracted to an illegal drug. Throughout history, there always has been some glamour attached to the underworld, bandits and thieves. At the simplest level, it is the fact that what they are doing is against the rules that attracts children to hide behind the bicycle sheds and smoke cigarettes. People will always want to rebel against society and I suspect that the persecution of drug users attracts as many people as it frightens. When American actor Stacey Keach was imprisoned in England in 1984, for carrying cocaine through customs, the newspaper coverage simply highlighted the fact that many American showbusiness personalities use cocaine as a regular habit.

Legislation to control the production and distribution of drugs needs to be tight and powerful but it is difficult to see what advantages are gained from arresting, fining and imprisoning addicts. Society is as unlikely to gain from imprisoning drug users as it is to gain from putting drunken tramps in prison.

The problems caused by turning drug users into martyrs and making a drug using habit seem rebellious and even glamorous are considerable. Even some members of the police force seem to agree with this point. In an article in the medical magazine *Update*, in 1982, Detective Inspector Jonathan P Bound, in charge of the Thames Valley Police Drug Squad, wrote: 'certainly a prison sentence is a suitable penalty for the unscrupulous dealer, but it serves no useful purpose whatsoever where the actual addict is concerned.'

Legislation's effect on usage

The main shortcoming of drug control legislation, however, is not that it is arbitrary or glamorises drug taking, but that it doesn't deal with the source of the problem: the forces which drive people to use drugs.

However much legislation is introduced and however many law enforcement officers are seconded to drug use control, the people who originally needed drugs will still need drugs. All the legislation does is either push the user into changing to an acceptable, legally available drug or into obtaining his drug through illegal sources.

Neither alternative is likely to make much difference to the user's health (presumably the original purpose of the exercise) and, indeed, both alternatives produce additional problems.

For most drug users, new legislation or the tightening up of old legislation means that they turn to the illegal drug market; the underground pushers and dealers who can be found all around the world selling drugs of all kinds and able to obtain just about any product as long as the price is right. The consequences of legislation, therefore, can be extremely damaging to the addict and to the society in which he lives.

By buying his drug supplies illegally the user changes his social status from law-abiding citizen to hunted criminal. For the first time in his life he will spend time with members of the underworld. He will pick up their habits and begin to associate with them and their ideals. Because the price of the drug will probably be high he may have difficulty in raising the necessary cash. The obvious solution will be to turn to crime: prostitution, thieving or drug pushing. In one study done in Philadelphia, in the United States of America, each addict in a group of 237 committed an average of 192 crimes every year in order to support his habit.

The real tragedy of much modern police activity is that it is too often leads to the arrest of the drug user rather than the supplier, who is usually well organised and difficult to catch. Suppliers handle huge quantities of drugs but are not themselves addicts and do not deal on the streets. They use aeroplanes or couriers to transport drugs and are well protected from the relatively short arm of the law. Those most likely to be arrested are the addicts and street pushers (themselves usually addicts).

Law enforcement officers around the world pursue drug users with zeal and laws created to help stamp out the distribution and sale of illegal drugs are often used to harass drug users. In Britain, the 1971 Act gave the police the right to stop, search and detain anyone reasonably suspected of possessing a controlled drug. The police also have the authority to burst into people's homes without warning if they suspect that there may be drugs on the premises. All this causes drug users to have contempt for the forces of law and order and to associate more and more with hardened members of the criminal fraternity. Because he is buying his drug supplies from an illegal source, the drug user is also quite likely to switch to another illegal drug. Once he has access to the drug underworld it is easy to find suppliers of other drugs. Some suppliers provide free samples in order to recruit new users. Although the number of heroin addicts is very small when compared to the number of cannabis users, all the evidence seems to show that just about every heroin user started off by using cannabis and graduated to heroin. (Schoolchildren heroin users are an exception to this general rule.) There isn't a physiological link between the use of cannabis and the use of heroin: the link is social. And whatever drug a user buys, there is always a risk that it will be contaminated. Buyers obtaining drugs illegally are in no position to complain about the strength or quality of the product they are purchasing.

The other risk that the drug user has to face when buying supplies illegally is that the type of drug he can obtain may be more dangerous than the drug he formerly used. So the hillworkers in the Andes turn from coca leaf to cocaine and the opium users of Hong Kong turn to heroin. In both cases the traditional, legal product was relatively safe and free of side effects. The modern equivalent – the only version readily obtainable illegally – is neither safe nor free from side effects.

Those are all hazards that the drug user who has to buy his drugs illegally must face. But even the drug user who changes to another, legal, drug may still be taking a risk. In China, for example, a massive campaign was launched in the 1950s to eliminate opium usage. Heavy legal controls were introduced and people suspected of using opium were locked up without trial. These controls worked reasonably well and huge numbers of opium users switched to a legal drug, tobacco. (The Chinese Government was happy to allow its citizens to smoke tobacco since the Chinese tobacco crop, which is the largest in the world, brings in foreign revenue.) Unhappily, the Chinese people soon started developing tobacco-induced health problems. The irony is that opium smoking is a relatively harmless habit and the Chinese people, encouraged by their law, had exchanged a relatively danger-free addiction for a lethal one.

Similarly, in India, people who have been denied access to alcohol have turned to imported drugs such as barbiturates and benzodiazepines. Again, they have replaced an illegal drug with a legal drug, but they have exchanged one type of danger for another. The law hasn't helped them at all.

Other dangers of legislation

So far I have only dealt with the direct dangers produced by legislation to control the use of drugs. But dividing drugs into two groups, those accepted legally and those not accepted legally, is bad for yet another reason: it encourages us to suppose that only illegal drugs are really hazardous or addictive.

During recent years I've met many benzodiazepine users who believe that the drug they have been taking must be free of risk because it is obtainable on prescription. It is quite common for men and women taking half-a-dozen Valium tablets a day to complain self-righteously about 'those terrible people who use drugs like heroin and cannabis'.

In truth, a number of drugs available on prescription are far more dangerous than drugs obtainable only through the black market. So this artificial division of drugs into 'legal' and 'illegal' groups can result in drug dangers being underestimated. This is yet another reason why we should think very carefully before increasing legislation to control drug usage. Indeed, I think that the evidence that is available suggests that we would probably benefit if we reduced the amount of legislation. One enormous advantage of this would be that the police and the courts would be removed from the picture.

At the moment, just about everyone involved in the process of law seems to have an opinion on why people become addicts, how they should be treated, what sort of punishments should be handed out and so on. Since law enforcement officers and lawyers are all trained to think in terms of 'crimes' and 'punishments' they tend to perpetuate the idea that all users of illegal drugs, being by definition criminals, must be punished. And they have very fixed ideas about just what those punishments should be. At Christmas 1984 the British Government introduced a 'Stay Low' campaign, to encourage more sensible drinking habits. The theory behind the campaign was that old-fashioned 'Don't drink and drive' slogans don't work because they are unrealistic and too authoritarian. It was hoped that this new campaign would work by educating people and offering them advice rather than orders. Unfortunately, a number of police forces in Britain decided that the campaign wasn't tough enough and didn't suit their ideas about how drinking drivers should be approached. As a result, some police forces refused to take part in the campaign or to use the posters and leaflets provided. Apart from the fact that it was surprising to see police authorities refusing to accept instruction from their Government, it was worrying to think where this type of police anarchy could lead.

The simplistic, traditional police approach may satisfy the narrow legal mind, but anyone who has worked with addicts or studied the problems of drug addiction will confirm that you cannot deal with addicts by throwing them into prison. Attempts to control them by legal means don't work because you have to care what happens to you to be usefully controlled in any legal way. Most addicts reach the point where they no longer care about anything other than obtaining supplies of their drug. Most skilled professional observers would probably agree that the existing laws make the problems worse by ensuring that addicts are isolated from other members of our society. During the last 50 years numerous attempts have been made to control drug use and drug addiction by introducing more and more legislation. The League of Nations and the United Nations have contrived to eradicate drug use. Individual governments all over the world have introduced drug control legislation. But throughout this time the size of the drug abuse problem has continued to grow. We should perhaps remember the lesson learned by the Americans during those sad years when prohibition was in force. The advantages of the legislative approach are extremely few; the disadvantages are numerous and important. After prohibition had ended in America the amount of alcohol being produced and consumed *fell* by 50 percent. It was the very fact that drinking was illegal that had proved so attractive to millions. I believe that these days so many people are determined to rebel that by increasing legislation we make drugs *more* attractive. In the long run the problems of drug addiction will only be ameliorated by improving the standard of the society in which we all live.

THE MEDICAL APPROACH

The technique used when a doctor is confronted with an addict who wants to kick his addiction depends on the addict, the doctor and the subject of the addiction. There is no such thing as a typical addict or even a typical heroin addict. Every case is different and so is every successful solution.

For all addicts, the first, and often most difficult step, is making the initial break from the addiction. This 'withdrawal' process can be uncomfortable, painful and even dangerous and an addict needs all the professional help he can get, mainly because with the right advice it is possible to minimise the effects of the withdrawal process.

The drug with which agonising withdrawal symptoms are most commonly associated is probably heroin. For years now, film directors have given us horrific images of heroin addicts going through the withdrawal stage; the standard picture is of an addict screaming with pain and struggling to cope with the most fearsome nightmares.

In practice, heroin withdrawal is rarely this horrendous. Most medical experts claim that the physical problems faced by a heroin addict kicking his habit are probably little worse than a bad attack of influenza. According to a report published in the journal *Medical News*, in July 1984, heroin addicts should be able to deal with the physical symptoms of withdrawal by using mild pain-killers, relaxation exercises, hot water bottles and plenty of warm baths.

The tragedy as far as heroin withdrawal is concerned is that during the last century or so doctors have frequently introduced withdrawal 'cures' for heroin which have in practice simply replaced one set of problems with another. The theory behind this sort of replacement therapy is that by giving a patient a safe and non-addictive drug it is possible to ease an addict through the pangs of withdrawal and minimise the unpleasant effects which can accompany the withdrawal process. In practice, the substances used to ease the withdrawal process usually cause as many problems as the original drug of addiction. Back in the 19th century, for example, doctors first advocated the use of morphine injections for the treatment of opium addicts, and then recommended heroin for the treatment of morphine addiction!

During the present century a wide range of products have been used as aids for addicts coming off heroin. Electro-convulsive therapy (in which electricity is pumped into the brain in the hope that it will have some useful effect on brain activity) has been tried, as has treatment with an enormous variety of drugs. However, the one product most commonly associated with heroin withdrawal is methadone, first introduced as a treatment for heroin addiction in America in 1964. At that time it was claimed that the drug was safe and that the side effects associated with it were few and mild.

It was argued that there were a number of important advantages in weaning patients off heroin with the aid of methadone.

It was claimed that methadone's long duration of action meant that addicts could be given a once-a-day dose of the drug in a specialist clinic. This would mean that the addicts themselves wouldn't need to be given drug supplies to take away with them.

It was claimed that because methadone didn't produce any tolerance, the addict would not need to increase his dose in order to obtain the same effect.

It was argued that methadone not only produced a fairly stable level of activity throughout the day but kept addicts satisfied without making them feel euphoric or 'high'. With these advantages in mind hundreds of doctors started using methadone to help addicts withdraw from heroin.

Sadly, however, within less than a decade it had become clear that by using methadone to help wean addicts off heroin all doctors did was to exchange one form of addiction for another. For example, by 1972 there were 80,000 methadone users in the United States of America. Today methadone addiction has joined heroin addiction as a major international drug problem. By using methadone doctors haven't helped their patients at all. Indeed, since there is now a black market trade in methadone it could be argued that doctors have made the addiction problem worse.

When it became clear that methadone wasn't the 'wonder' drug it was first thought to be, doctors tried using other products to help their heroin addicts.

Propoxyphene (an analgesic derived from methadone but thought to be less addictive) turned out to be addictive too, and to be potentially fatal if mixed with alcohol.

Huge doses of Vitamin C didn't help very much either, and led to a tendency to develop kidney stones.

Naxalone produced such unpleasant symptoms that it was of very little practical value.

Clonidine (a drug originally used for the treatment of high blood pressure) not only produced blood pressure problems but also some psychiatric problems.

Between my writing down this information and you reading it, someone somewhere will have produced yet another drug; and will probably have declared it both safe and non-addictive. But the chances are high that within a year or so that drug will produce problems and may even have addictive qualities of its own.

General practitioners' role

The message that comes through from all this seems to be that doctors can help their addicts most by helping them to withdraw from drug use completely. Drug withdrawal techniques which involve the use of a substitute drug rarely provide long-term answers – the only advantage being that an addict may be able to obtain his replacement drugs legally instead of illegally.

Most of these experiments with drugs designed to ease the pains of withdrawal have been designed and organised by specialists working in hospitals or specially funded clinics. But the medical practitioner most likely to be consulted by an addict needing help will be a general practitioner rather than a specialist.

And in some ways the general practitioner is theoretically the most useful professional as far as the addict is concerned. If an addict sees his own family doctor he will probably be seeing someone whom he has known for a considerable time; someone in whom he has trust and who should be skilled at developing and maintaining a good, solid personal relationship with him. The general practitioner will probably have a surgery that is fairly close. He will have daily surgeries and be available at most times of the day for emergency consultations and he should have the time and the skills required to help the addict get through the withdrawal period as comfortably and safely as possible.

Unfortunately, it is relatively rare for general practitioners to be willing to spend time working with addicts. There are several reasons for this.

Doctors in general practice are usually rather frightened of drug addicts, for a number of quite good reasons. Their main worry is that they will acquire a reputation for helping addicts and will end up with a queue of difficult and demanding patients. Very few addicts are willing to give up their drugs. Most addicts will expect to be given supplies of the drug they use – even if they are determined to cut down. The doctor fears than once he starts prescribing an addictive drug he will be inundated with requests from other local addicts.

And he worries that by prescribing for an addict he may attract the attention of the local police or national regulatory bodies, some of which in recent years have taken a very strong line with doctors who deal kindly with addicts. Also, most doctors know very well that addicts tend to be violent on occasion, and that they will lie in order to obtain drug supplies.

Doctors know, too, that addicts need much time and attention. Generally speaking, they are not cost-effective patients – unless a doctor is prepared just to hand over drug prescriptions in exchange for cash.

Next, doctors tend to share an enormous burden of guilt over the whole subject of drug addiction. After all, it is the medical profession which has produced some of the major drug addiction problems of the 1980s. It was doctors overprescribing barbiturates that gave us the barbiturate problem. Similarly, overprescribing of amphetamines and benzodiazepines produced those particular difficulties. Astonishingly, general practitioners often find the addiction problem so difficult to accept that they will deny its very existence or importance.

Finally, doctors simply don't know how to cope. Medical training rarely includes much information on drug addiction and doctors often feel incompetent and bewildered when face to face with a drug addict.

In an attempt to deal with all these problems, and help British general practitioners, in 1984 the British Medical Working Group on Drug Dependence produced a booklet entitled *Guidelines of Good Clinical Practice in the Treatment of Drug Misuse*. This was distributed to doctors throughout Britain and was intended as a practical handbook.

Unfortunately, the Working Group seems to have suffered from too much close contact with British bureaucrats for it produced a pretty unreadable and unusable document which probably ended up in filing cabinets and even waste-paper baskets. I find it difficult to believe that more than a handful of general practitioners read the document or learned from it anything of value.

Indeed, that may not be a bad thing for the document contains some surprising information. For example, the Working Group claims that 'Definite withdrawal symptoms are often seen in patients abruptly stopping benzodiazepines taken in normal dose for longer than 3 to 4 months.' Some experts would consider that a gross overestimate of the time it takes to become addicted to benzodiazepines.

It does seem a pity that the one official attempt to encourage general practitioners to help drug addicts should be so feeble and ineffective. For all the evidence suggests that when general practitioners are encouraged to take an interest in drug addiction they can play an extremely effective role in helping addicts to kick their habit.

Helping the smoker

The evidence suggests that no one individual is more likely to be able to help a smoker give up his tobacco than a general practitioner.

Usually, when smokers try to give up their habit they succeed only for a short time. Something like 80 percent of smokers who give up after visiting an acupuncturist or a hypnotist, or after attending a special class for would-be non-smokers, will be puffing away again within months. Two-thirds of the smokers who give up will be smoking again within three months. But when smokers are given help and encouragement by their general practitioner they have a much higher permanent success rate. Between a third and a half of all the smokers who give up with their doctor's help are completely successful. That's a pretty impressive track record.

Some general practitioners help their patients simply by providing encouragement, support and motivation. Others prescribe products such as nicotine chewing gum – a substance introduced in 1980 and said by some general practitioners to be a valuable aid for smokers anxious to give up their habit. The chewing gum enables the smoker to reduce his dosage of nicotine slowly without smoking at all. In Britain the one problem with nicotine chewing gum is that although on a number of occasions it has been shown to be effective, the Department of Health and Social Security has consistently refused to accept it as a necessary drug suitable for providing on a National Health Service prescription.

Helping the alcoholic

General practitioners as a group have been particularly successful in helping patients to stop smoking. Some have also been fairly successful with alcoholics. Here, one of the most effective treatments has involved the use of drugs such as disulfiram (often prescribed as Antabuse). This product has been available as a treatment for alcoholics for about a quarter of a century, and although expert opinion on its value seems divided, there are enthusiastic general practitioners who claim that it works extremely well. The drug works by blocking the metabolism of alcohol and although there is a wide variation in the way that individuals respond, some doctors have had considerable success with it.

The technique involved is fairly simple. The doctor gives the patient tablets to take (or surgically implants a supply of the drug in the patient's stomach) and warns the patient that if he drinks he will become ill. The effectiveness of the product depends mainly on the individual's determination to stop drinking. A well-motivated patient who really wants to give up alcohol will benefit as long as he keeps taking the tablets regularly. If he drinks after taking the tablets he will become ill – usually sweating, flushing, developing a tight chest, fainting and vomiting. All those symptoms can develop after just a sip of alcohol.

Hospitals, clinics and residential centres

General practitioners do have an important role to play in the treatment of drug addiction. And I believe, they could play a far more important role if they were better educated and encouraged to spend more time dealing with addicts. But for many addicts – and in particular those who have taken physically debilitating drugs such as heroin, or those whose addic-

tion has led them into a homeless and largely illegal existence – professional help will mean a hospital, a specialist
clinic or some form of residential centre. There, experts can
provide physical, psychological and social support, as well as
protection from pushers and officers of the law.

In many residential centres the experts involved usually
include a number of former addicts who know at first hand
exactly what the addict is going through.

There is a good deal of evidence to show that, when
properly organised, these centres can play an important part
in the treatment of people taking drugs such as heroin. (It
isn't the fact that they have been on heroin that results in
their need for this type of professional support so much as the
fact that by the very illegal nature of the drug they are using
heroin addicts tend to be homeless, frightened, unemployed
and lonely.) A good residential centre can offer accommo-
dation, medical treatment for infections and other physical
problems, counselling, group support, decent food and
friendship. Addicts do benefit when provided with a structured lifestyle, a purpose and some responsibility.

The tragedy is, however, that there are nowhere near
enough residential centres for all the addicts who need help.
In Britain, in 1984, there were an estimated 84 officially
available beds for addicts. At the time when that estimate
was printed in *The Times* it was widely thought that there were
50–60,000 addicts in the country. Nor did the Government
seem to have any plans to increase the number of residential
beds. For most addicts the only hope of finding residential care
is either to have relatives rich enough to pay for private treatment (which can be excellent but also horrifically expensive) or
to have access to a centre run by a voluntary organisation.

Alternative forms of treatment

So far in this chapter I have dealt only with the help provided
by orthodox medical services. There are, however, a number
of unorthodox or 'alternative' forms of treatment available
for addicts of various kinds and for the sake of completeness
these need to be mentioned.

Acupuncture, for example, is quite widely advocated as a treatment for many types of addiction – including smoking and eating too much. Similarly a number of hypnotists claim that they can help addicts, too. My own feeling is that there is as yet absolutely no convincing evidence to show that either of these 'alternative' treatments have any real value.

Behaviour therapy is the one alternative form of treatment that does seem to have some real value. At its very simplest level, this type of treatment depends on giving an individual praise when he does well and telling him off or punishing him when he fails. Parents use behaviour therapy all the time. When they tell their children off for not eating all their food they are effectively training them to empty their plates when they sit down to a meal. (This type of destructive behaviour therapy is actually responsible for many bad eating habits – see page 92.)

Pet owners use 'behaviour' therapy too. They shout at their puppy or kitten when it makes a mess on the kitchen floor and they praise it lovingly when it uses the appropriate sand tray.

Aversion therapy is the type of behaviour therapy used most commonly for addicts. The patient is gradually taught to associate his addiction with punishment or pain of some kind. This treatment has been adopted by many orthodox practitioners and is used by doctors in a number of hospitals and centres. For example, it is fairly commonly used in the treatment of alcoholics. After being given a drug such as disulfiram (see page 147) the alcoholic will be given a drink of alcohol. The combination will make him extremely sick. The theory is that if the alcoholic is subjected to this type of unpleasant experience often enough then he will eventually develop a genuine dislike for alcohol. And he'll stop drinking.

All these treatment techniques have their supporters.

Importance of self-motivation and personal circumstances

There are some people who believe that the real answers to our addiction problem lie in the hands of general practitioners. Others argue that if we are to see the problem solved effectively we must allocate more financial resources to building specialist centres for the treatment of addicts. Some believe that orthodox medicine has all the answers. Others claim that alternative practitioners have the most effective solutions.

Personally, I feel that general practitioners, hospital specialists and some alternative practitioners all have roles to play in the treatment of drug addiction but that none of these experts can hope to cure an addict without first ensuring that the addict is thoroughly motivated to give up his addiction and then ensuring that his social and personal circumstances are changed so that his need for outside support is reduced.

Getting an addict properly motivated is one of the first things that has to be done if a withdrawal programme is to be successful. Without his enthusiastic support and determination any technique is almost bound to fail. It is, in part at least, the doctor's responsibility to help produce the right sort of motivation.

Motivation can come from many sources and in many guises. An illness caused by his addiction may finally strike home and encourage an addict to change his lifestyle. Over 60 percent of smokers with a related disease can be persuaded to give up smoking completely and another 20 percent can be persuaded to cut down appreciably. A pregnancy, birthday, new job offer, courtship or promise of a new home can also act as motivating forces.

There are probably as many different motivating forces as there are addicts.

Once an addict is properly motivated then there is an excellent chance that he can be helped. But unless the addict's social circumstances can be improved, and his personal problems resolved to a certain extent, then the chances of the addict obtaining any long-term help are still slim. Once again, helping to improve an addict's personal circumstances must be a medical responsibility.

Something like four out of every five heroin addicts start using the drug again within 12 months of successfully finishing a withdrawal programme. They don't start using heroin again because their physical addiction has remained intolerable and irresistible, but because their problems and their surroundings haven't changed and so the solutions they choose don't change.

Much the same sort of thing is true of smokers. The majority of people who give up smoking start again before many months are over, not due to a continuing addiction to tobacco, but because their problems and stresses haven't changed and they haven't found an alternative solution. Too many so-called experts seem to forget that it isn't a drug alone that causes an addiction. To be successful a treatment programme must be aimed more at the individual addict than at the addiction he has acquired.

If an addict is helped to kick his drug habit and then thrown back into his old environment then the chances are very high that he will start using drugs again. He will mix with the same people, collect the same bad habits and probably find himself being pressured by the same pushers, and the same demands. He may even find himself being harassed by the same police officers. All this will make a successful rehabilitation nigh on impossible. If, however, an addict can be resettled, given a home, a job and a new, legal lifestyle then his chances of remaining off drugs are much greater. During the Vietnam war large numbers of soldiers became addicted to heroin while they were in Vietnam. A year later, back in the United States, many managed to kick their heroin habit with remarkably little trouble.

Helping the addict cope with his personal problems and pressures is equally important. Patients who are given narcotic drugs for pain relief become dependent on those drugs for just as long as the pain continues, but when the pain disappears then so will their craving for the drug. Much the same is true of other pressures too. On pages 103 to 128 I discussed some of the commonest reasons why people get addicted. Two of the commonest are boredom and pressure. If an individual who started using drugs because of pressure returns home after treatment and finds himself under exactly the same pressure then the chances are that he will succumb to the same addiction. Similarly, an addict who started using drugs because he was bored will be quite likely to start using drugs again if he returns home after successfully 'kicking' his habit only to find himself stuck back in the same, boring routine. Over 100 years ago it was shown quite conclusively that when patients in mental hospitals are provided with proper employment their need for sedative drugs is reduced fairly dramatically. But that lesson is still ignored by many of today's doctors and administrators. We still tend to regard addictions as illnesses, and symptoms as problems which require outside therapy. We prefer to spend money on drugs and treatment programmes rather than on teaching people how to survive, how to deal with stress and pressure and how to create for themselves a fruitful and rewarding lifestyle.

If an addict is going to give up his addiction permanently something will have to be added to his original lifestyle. The impulse that produced the addiction will have to be channelled into something safer, more useful and more rewarding. His social status and his personal circumstances will have to be improved.

Most addicts start using drugs because they need to hide from the real world. If they stop using drugs but then return to the same cruel, unbearable world, they will inevitably start using drugs again.

And we have to remember, too, that no two addicts are the same and so no two solutions can be the same either. People become addicted for a huge variety of different reasons. Indeed we all respond to drugs in different ways. You can see the truth in this statement simply by looking around you at the next social event you attend. Just see what happens when people start drinking alcohol. Some will become aggressive, some will become jolly and funny, a few will become drowsy, others will become rude and even lascivious. What is true of alcohol is equally true of all other drugs.

Supporting the addict

Finally, it is also vitally important to remember that when an addict has been using a drug for some time he will probably have forgotten how to respond to normal social and personal problems. For however long he has been addicted he will have been using drugs to avoid personal confrontations; he will have been hiding behind a pharmacological barrier. Without his drug support he will be exceptionally vulnerable to all physical, mental, moral, spiritual and emotional pressures. He will need a good deal of love, sympathy and patience from those around him.

Inevitably, few of these needs can be met through traditional medical services. Today there are too many addicts with problems needing too much time and support. People who become addicts are vulnerable and often emotionally unstable. They are frequently immature and invariably sensitive to stress and pressure. They need far more help than doctors, hospitals or clinics can provide.

The major causes of disease these days are stress, pressure and boredom. And the major consequence of those threats is addiction of one sort or another. The problem is too large for medicine to solve. And, anyway, medicine has relatively few answers. I believe that the solution to this 20th-century plague lies within those voluntary organisations which exist to teach addicts and their friends and their relatives how best to cope themselves.

Addictions have proved to be one of the greatest threats to life in the 20th century. It is ironic that at a time when scientific medicine is improving faster than at any previous period in history, the answer to this major threat will come not from any orthodox healing group but from volunteers and sufferers themselves. For a century or more the medical profession has conspired to take away our responsibility for our own health. But now, through organisations like Alcoholics Anonymous, we are learning that we will only find true and lasting solutions to these problems by taking the responsibility for our own health.

THE UNOFFICIAL APPROACH

For years, the main burden of caring for addicts has been shouldered by their long-suffering relatives and friends. It is they who have found the time and patience, mental strength, physical strength and financial resources to offer help and support. With the normal sense of compassion that we all feel when we see someone whom we love and care for suffering and in torment, these people have sacrificed their own lives, careers, homes and health. Often they have ignored the appeals and warnings of others and have thrown away their lives in what is not only a thankless task but all too often a fruitless one.

It is often fruitless for the simple reason that the addict is probably beyond that sort of help. When someone has become an addict he won't usually respond to the old-fashioned, traditional values. You can't get through to him with love, with affection, with caring or even with guilt. You can't buy his freedom with money or time or any valuable resource. Addicts live in a world where their needs, ambitions, fears and desires are ruled not by normal human emotions but by physical and psychological needs produced by their addiction.

Relatives and friends usually take a long time to learn this valuable lesson. And it is always a lesson that has to be learned the hard way. When someone close to you is in despair it is natural to offer help, friendship and trust, and to keep on doing so even when the only reward is continual, cruel betrayal.

You can never cure an addict with love and friendship alone. But no caring relative ever believes that, until both love and friendship have been taken to the very limits of their endurance and stretched to – and sometimes beyond – breaking point.

(For advice on how you *can* help an addict, see page 165.)

Self-help groups
In the past, when the breaking point was reached the relative

or friend would invariably move out and move away. He or she would have tried the usual resources and found them sadly wanting. Doctors and others experienced at working with addicts are too battle-weary and scarred to offer their trust and friendship. Most important of all there are far too few professional resources or specialist clinics to offer all addicts proper clinical help and guidance.

Today, however, there *is* hope and there *is* help available. It comes not from any orthodox, established source. It comes neither from orthodox medicine, nor from alternative or complementary medicine. It doesn't even come from dispassionate, caring volunteers. It comes from a unique type of self-help group; the type of group formed by addicts for addicts, who themselves know the heartaches and pains. And who, perhaps most important of all, know that for an addict to give up his addiction successfully he must both recognise that he has a problem and sincerely want to be free of it.

Self-help groups have been a remarkably successful feature of 20th-century life and have played an important part in the treatment of addicts of all kinds. By far the largest and most successful group has been Alcoholics Anonymous, an organisation that is still only half a century old but now has well over a million members spread through numerous groups in over 100 countries.

Alcoholics Anonymous originated in a chance meeting that took place back in 1935 in Akron, Ohio, between Robert Holbrook Smith, a local doctor, and William Wilson, a New York stockbroker. In 1934 Wilson had attended the Oxford Group Movement after a friend had told him that he had successfully managed to stay sober by attending their group discussion meetings. William Wilson explained to Dr Smith that the meetings involved group members in an open confession during which they talked about their emotional problems, shared past experiences and together prayed to God.

Both Smith and Wilson were anxious to control drinking and used the basic principles of the Oxford Group Movement discussion group as a starting point. They found that when a drinker talked about his experiences in trying to give up alcohol, his desire to drink was much easier to control.

They next introduced this new concept to a number of other local drinkers, in particular those alcoholics incarcerated on the wards of the Akron City Hospital. It was there that they formulated their now famous 'twelve steps for recovery' and founded the organisation Alcoholics Anonymous. Right from the start the only requirement for membership was an honest desire to stop drinking.

Since those early days Smith and Wilson's formula has hardly changed. Alcoholics Anonymous doesn't claim to cure alcoholism but aims to help end the problems so commonly associated with the excessive use of alcohol. As one AA member succinctly put it, 'we sober up drunks and keep them sober'.

Belief in a god, or at least in a superior being of some kind, is an essential part of the AA philosophy. They talk to one another, share experiences, help each other with support and offer hope through example. One of the tenets of their faith is to concentrate on keeping sober for one day at a time and they deliberately keep their aims and ambitions simple, sharing a determination to take each day as it comes. They organise meetings for friends and relatives and for members of the public too, but their most important meetings – at which alcoholics can share their burdens with others who understand – are held behind closed doors and in total anonymity. On their shared faith they slowly rebuild their lives, replacing guilt, shame and remorse with purposefulness and self-respect. Each meeting ends with a simple prayer: 'God grant me the serenity to accept the things I cannot change, courage to change the things I can and wisdom to know the difference.'

During the last 10 years or so the membership of Alcoholics Anonymous has increased dramatically – with nearly half of the new members being women. As a result, these days there can't be many alcoholics who are more than an hour or so away from their nearest branch of AA. Amazingly, only one in six of the new members who join come because they are recommended to do so by their doctors. The rest turn up simply because they have heard of the effectiveness of the organisation and because they have a problem that no one else has been able to help them solve.

Most doctors who specialise in the treatment of alcoholics work closely with AA and there seems little doubt that the organisation has done more than any profession, statutory body or other voluntary organisation to help the lot of the alcoholic. The organisation's literature is now available in numerous languages, and in braille, but despite its international success AA has always managed to avoid allying itself with any moral, ethical, religious or political views. It never gets involved in anything that could be considered controversial or contentious.

Alcoholics Anonymous has, however, done far more than just help alcoholics. During the last few years it has spawned a whole series of similar organisations which provide help and support both for addicts and for their friends and relatives. There is, for example, the organisation Al-Anon, which offers help, support and advice to the relatives and friends of alcoholics. And there is Alateen, the teenage counterpart of Al-Anon, an organisation which offers a programme of support to teenagers affected by someone else's drinking.

Alcoholics Anonymous has even had an influence away from the specific problem of drinking, inspiring the foundation of other organisations with a philosophy very much akin to that of the older organisation.

For people who are addicted to gambling there is Gamblers Anonymous.

For those addicted to food there is Overeaters Anonymous.

All these organisations are independent but they all have much in common: they emphasise the need to rely on one another's strengths and on some form of supernatural power, some undefined and undefinable Force. They are all organisations which are run by sufferers for sufferers, and they illustrate perfectly the power of self-help and self-healing.

I think that the enormous strength of these organisations is that they *don't* offer any magical solutions and they *don't* offer to take over any individual's problems.

One major weakness of orthodox treatments for addiction is that when the addict is taken into a rehabilitation unit of a hospital he is encouraged to hand over all his fears, worries and problems to someone else. He is encouraged to put all his faith in an outsider; to allow a doctor or a nurse to take responsibility for his life.

This provides the addict with immediate, temporary solace but it doesn't provide him with any long-term solutions. It invariably means that when the addict's treatment period is complete he will be left more vulnerable than ever, more exposed and more susceptible to temptation. He will have had no opportunity to build up his strength or deal with his problem himself. In addition, those who have taken the responsibility for his addiction away from him will have given him a constant excuse for continued failure.

Organisations such as Alcoholics Anonymous work for the very simple reason that they encourage addicts to gain strength through taking control of their own lives and they provide a continuing framework upon which the individual can build his self-control. The Alcoholics Anonymous organisation doesn't throw an addict out into the cold, cruel world when he has managed to break free of his addiction. The AA organisation will always be there, week in and week out. And the other members of AA, who together provide succour and support, advice and encouragement, will be there too. The self-help groups provide continuing evidence for the success of their own philosophy.

I think that self-help groups such as the ones I've mentioned (and there are many such organisations providing help for sufferers from just about every type of addiction and every type of personal problem) offer far more than any official bodies or professional groups can ever hope to offer. I think that these organisations work because their members not only understand the problems and pressures which exist but because they also care and they offer one another both motivation and a community spirit that can be truly healing.

Self-help groups and preventive strategies

Up until fairly recently, self-help organisations dealt only with addicts, their families and their friends. In the last few years, however, there has been a departure from this traditional approach and today self-help groups are moving into the world of preventive medicine. For example, there is now an organisation called Drinkwatchers which provides advice and help to people who realise that they are beginning to drink too much but who have not yet become alcoholics. By suggesting that drinkers keep a diary of their drinking habits, plan out social situations and learn how to say 'no' to excess drinks, Drinkwatchers should enable many to keep their social drinking under control. By linking that practical advice with a community spirit and a real sense of purpose they may well enable their members to survive in a world where addiction to drugs of one sort or another is becoming more and more often the unhealthy solution to the pressure of the 20th century.

5

PRESCRIPTIONS
FOR THE FUTURE

In our desperate attempts to deal with the plague of addiction we have made a number of fundamental mistakes. We have assumed that when people become addicted their primary problem is a medical one, and we have organised our attempts to deal with them accordingly. The truth is that an addiction is a symptom not a disease; and it is a symptom of a social problem, not a medical problem. If we treat an addiction, we remove the symptoms but the basic problem remains unchanged. It is hardly surprising, therefore, if the symptoms come back.

Similarly, we have made the mistake of assuming that when the symptoms of an addiction differ then the treatment that is needed must differ too. The truth is that all types of addiction are symptoms and consequences of a relatively limited number of fairly identical basic problems.

It is through these fundamental errors that we have arrived at our second major misconception: that there must be a medical or a legal solution to the problem of addiction. This misconception has led us to make a number of important mistakes. For example, in our search for medical cures for addiction we have produced a more sophisticated, powerful and dangerous variety of drugs to which people can become addicted.

Ironically, during this century doctors have made the

addiction problem far worse than it would have been if we had not had a medical profession at all. Similarly, through our attempts to eradicate addiction by legal means we have again made things worse; our attempts have exacerbated the underlying social problems of alienation, frustration, loneliness and fear.

If we are going to deal effectively with our current addiction problem, help those who are already addicted and reduce the number of individuals becoming addicted in the future then we have to change our approach in a number of fundamental ways. If we don't make these changes, the size of the addiction problem will continue to grow at a dramatic rate for, as the natural stresses and pressures such as boredom and frustration increase, so will the need for artificial solutions of one sort or another. As economic policies lead to more and more unemployment so increasing numbers will seek release through drugs.

The first step must be to rethink our legislative approach to the whole problem of addiction. At the moment our controls persecute addicts as much as suppliers. Indeed, the natural vulnerability of the addict means that it is he and not the dealer or supplier who usually ends up in court. No addict is likely to be helped by punishment. Nor, indeed, is any other addict or user likely to be put off by the threat of punishment. We must therefore remove the addict from the legal target area and tighten the laws relating to the manufacture and sale of drugs.

Some of the most potent and destructive of drugs are manufactured and sold entirely legally. Our laws have become weak and flabby because there are too many huge international corporations making money out of addicts. We should concentrate our legal firepower on those who manufacture and sell products such as alcohol, tobacco, tranquillisers and heroin.

It is, for example, now clear that one of the major reasons for the increase in alcoholism during the last decade has been the wider availability of alcohol in shops and supermarkets. In Britain there are strict limits on the times that public houses can open – and keeping to these opening times does reduce drinking. But supermarkets and shops sell alcohol all day long. Making alcohol more readily available in this way leads to more drinking, and to more drinking at home. It makes life particularly difficult for anyone who is trying to give up or cut down on alcohol. We should trade in those laws which enable policemen to lock up drunks and replace them with stricter controls on those selling alcohol. It wouldn't please the industry and it might make the policeman's job harder but it would considerably reduce our alcohol problem.

Similarly, we should do more to control the sale of cigarettes. In 1984, an official Government survey on *Smoking Among Secondary Schoolchildren* showed that in Britain children aged 11 to 16 spend some £60 million a year on cigarettes. Nearly all the children involved bought their cigarettes from shops, despite the fact that it is an offence under the *Children and Young Persons Act* of 1933 to sell cigarettes to a child under the age of 16 years. The laws are there but they are not applied. Instead of arresting cannabis users the police should be arresting shopkeepers found guilty of selling cigarettes illegally. That, after all, is drug dealing and deserves severe punishment. I would suggest that any shopkeeper found selling cigarettes to a child under the age of 16 should be banned from selling tobacco at all.

While tightening up the laws relating to the sale of tobacco and alcohol we should also tighten up the laws which govern the sale of prescription drugs. If Britain would allow the World Health Organization to ban heroin then anyone holding commercial supplies of the drug would be liable to arrest. It wouldn't be possible for companies to manufacture heroin legally and so one source of supplies would dry up straight away.

We should also introduce more controls on the manufacture and sale of tranquillisers and other drugs likely to prove addictive. During the last couple of decades international drug companies have shown absolutely no sense of responsibility and, indeed, have sold their addictive drugs with tremendous vigour. All drugs having an effect on the mind should be controlled more closely by law.

One of the great anomalies of our current drug laws is that there are very few restrictions on drugs such as the benzodiazepines, whereas there is extremely powerful legislation controlling the use of such relatively harmless drugs as raw coca leaves, cannabis plants and even opium in its crudest state. It would make good sense to legalise these plants – they are all relatively harmless and the genuine problem their refined products create is minute compared to the size of the problem produced by tobacco, alcohol and the benzodiazepines. Legal controls have produced a black market and now threaten to turn a minor problem into a major threat. If we legalise opium, but tax it at an extremely high rate and put onerous restrictions on its manufacture and sale, then the popularity of heroin would decline. The real irony is that if people need temporary pharmacological aids, they would be better off using cannabis or coca leaves than tranquillisers or tobacco. Our drug legislation is totally absurd and quite out of date.

Our second major target for reform must be the medical profession. Here the irony is that doctors probably could help our drug addiction problem by retiring en masse and taking up carpentry or basket weaving. Failing that unlikely solution, we must encourage doctors to take more care over their use of drugs, to prescribe more hesitantly and to look more critically at new products.

Unfortunately, I can't see the medical profession taking very kindly to any of these suggestions. For 10 years now I've been writing about the problems caused by bad prescribing and have on several occasions forecast that if doctors won't control their use of drugs, control must be introduced by the Government. I think that the time has now come for action. Such controls will be opposed by doctors and there will be much talk about 'prescribing freedoms' and 'patients' rights', but I don't think we can afford to take notice of such bleatings. The medical profession has failed to deal responsibly with drugs and it must now be controlled by strictly applied legislation.

The huge amounts of money that will be saved by cutting back on our drug bills can then be spent on funding more self-help groups. It would be possible to reduce the NHS drugs bill in Britain by at least five hundred million pounds a year, simply by encouraging doctors to be more sensible in their prescribing habits. No patient need suffer from such cutbacks and if the savings are used to develop a larger network of self-help community groups (along the lines of the already vastly successful and independent Alcoholics Anonymous), the benefits would be enormous and long lasting. Funds can also be directed towards developing relaxation classes and providing people with advice on ways to deal with stress.

I think it is this final area which will have the greatest impact on the size of our addiction problem. The single biggest reason why so many millions turn to drugs and other aids is stress and pressure. By teaching people how to cope with them we will reduce the need for people to escape from their stresses with the aid of drugs. By changing our attitudes towards legislation and medical intervention we can reduce the pressures on addicts; by teaching people how best to survive in the maelstrom of 20th-century life we can reduce the number of people who need to turn to drugs at all.

But in the end, the size of our addiction problem will depend not on doctors or lawyers nor, I suspect, on the quality of self-help groups. It will depend on the quality of our society and on the ease with which citizens can retain their pride and self-respect. If economic policies are allowed to produce growing unemployment then, as the social structure of our society deteriorates, so the number of new addicts will continue to increase. As machines replace men and social security benefits replace wage packets, so the general level of frustration, boredom and guilt will rise and the need to escape become greater and more universal. Opium use in the 19th century only faded away as social conditions improved. The various addictions which now scar the late 20th century will only be defeated by politicians who care for and understand the needs and fragility of the human mind.

APPENDIX

HELPING AN ADDICT

1. You can't help an addict until he admits that he has a problem and confesses that he needs help.

2. Don't try to support or protect an addict who still refuses to seek help. You will merely prolong the agony. Don't make excuses for him or help him with his work.

3. Don't allow an addict's problem to take over your life. Do not give up your job or friends so that you can look after him or her. You will need all the outside strength and support you can muster if you are to survive.

4. If you give an addict an ultimatum then stick to it. Don't threaten to leave if he doesn't stop – and then feel sorry for him and change your mind. The addict is weak-willed and driven by his addiction; you need to be strong, determined and unwavering.

5. Offer as much support, encouragement and love as you can muster. If you care about what happens then make that clear. Try to boost his self esteem and self confidence by reminding him of his virtues and strengths. Do this repeatedly.

6. Never nag or moan and don't waste time and energy hunting for and destroying hidden supplies. You are

unlikely to change an addict's will or intentions by behaving in this way but you will damage an already fragile relationship.

7. Give support but do not allow yourself to become a prop or crutch. An addict needs to regain his own strength if he is to 'kick' his addiction successfully.

8. Any addict 'kicking' a habit should have medical help to start with. If medical or specialist help is available then try to make sure that the addict attends every appointment that is made for him.

9. Never offer what may seem to you to be a 'safe' alternative. Thousands of people have tried to help addicts withdrawing from benzodiazepines by offering different but similar drugs – and have simply produced a new problem to replace the old one.

10. Get the names and addresses of all local voluntary groups which may be able to offer help and support. Find out where and when meetings are held and do your best to ensure that your addict is able to attend all appropriate meetings. But don't try and force him to attend. Sort out transport problems if you can but don't try 'dragging' him to a meeting if he really doesn't want to go. Remember that neither you nor anyone else can help an addict until he admits that he has a problem and confesses that he needs help.

EMERGENCIES

1. Make sure that you have the telephone numbers and addresses of your own doctor and the addict's own doctor. You should also make sure that you know which local hospitals deal with medical emergencies – and when any local hospitals are closed.

2. Learn some basic first aid. Addicts are exceptionally prone to accidental injury. Attend a local first aid course if you can. If you can't, then borrow a book on first aid from your local library.

3. In any emergency telephone for help as soon as possible if you are at all uncertain about your ability to cope. Don't just wait to see how things go. Telephone the patient's general practitioner and/or the ambulance service.

4. Addicts can become physically dangerous. If you are frightened or think that you or anyone else could be harmed, get away as soon as you can and telephone the police, the addict's doctor and the ambulance service (in that order) as soon as you can.

5. If you ever have difficulty in reaching an addict's own general practitioner then telephone the general practitioner with whom you are registered. Remember that when you are away from home you are entitled to telephone any general practitioner for emergency help. Always try to telephone the patient's general practitioner first – rather than your own general practitioner. He will have access to important clinical information about the patient's past medical history. Besides, your own general practitioner will probably be unwilling to attend another doctor's patient (unless he knows that you have tried – and failed – to reach the patient's own doctor).

6. If you find someone unconscious do not stop to try and find out why he is unconscious. First, check to see if he is bleeding. If he is, then stop the bleeding by applying pressure directly to the wound. Make a pad with any piece of clean cloth and press on it. Tie it in place (for a minute or two only) or get someone else (even a child) to keep pressing while you telephone for help. Keep pressing until help arrives.

7. If you find someone who isn't breathing, loosen the clothes around his neck, remove any blockage from his

mouth (food, vomit or false teeth) and provide artificial respiration. Lie him on his back, tilt his head backwards, pinch his nostrils and blow air into his mouth 12 times a minute. Between breaths shout for someone to telephone for an ambulance.

8. If you find a patient unconscious but breathing normally, put him into the 'coma' position. He should be on his left side with his right knee drawn up towards his chest.

9. If your patient is choking, stand behind him with your arms clasped tightly around his upper abdomen. Then squeeze tightly and quickly. Before attempting this manoeuvre remove any food that remains in his mouth.

10. Don't try to restrain a patient who is having a fit. Loosen any tight clothing and remove any false teeth. Put a rolled up handkerchief or empty glove between his teeth to prevent injury to his tongue. (Do not use a spoon – this can result in broken teeth.) The safest place for a patient having a fit is on the floor. Move away anything on which he could injure himself. Keep him lying on his side rather than on his front or back. Make sure that he doesn't swallow his tongue – pull it forward if necessary. Stay with him until he has recovered consciousness. Ring the patient's general practitioner or an ambulance as soon as you can.

11. Unless you know exactly what you are doing, do not try moving someone who has injured himself. Deal with bleeding or provide artificial respiration if necessary. Put him into the 'coma' position if he is unconscious. But then telephone for an ambulance and/or his general practitioner.

12. Burns are best dealt with by immersing the burnt area in cold water for at least five minutes. If the burn covers more than an inch or two or looks severe, then telephone the patient's general practitioner and/or an ambulance.

13. Addicts suffering from mental symptoms (confusion,

depression, hallucinations or delusions) need urgent medical help. Do not try to deal with any of these problems yourself but telephone the patient's general practitioner straight away.

14. Alternative medical practitioners can help patients in many different ways. But I do not know of any alternative practitioners offering a full 24-hour a day 'emergency' service for patients. And I know of no alternative practitioners who claim to be able to treat all emergencies. Remember also that alternative practitioners will not have access to hospital casualty units or psychiatric units.

WITHDRAWAL/GIVING UP AN ADDICTION

1. By definition anyone who 'gives up' an addiction will have to go through a period of 'withdrawal' which will probably be uncomfortable, unpleasant and even painful.

2. The length of time for which these symptoms last will depend upon the health and physical make up of the individual concerned, on the length of time for which he has been taking his drug and on the dosage he has been taking.

3. Withdrawal symptoms for identical substances vary from one individual to another. One addict may manage to give up a drug with a modest number of relatively mild side effects. Another addict may suffer from an entirely different set of symptoms.

4. Because the symptoms may be disturbing, any addict planning to give up his addiction should be in a quiet, peaceful place when starting his withdrawal. Outside pressures and stresses need to be kept to an absolute minimum.

5. Before withdrawing from a drug an addict should seek medical advice. Some drugs (such as barbiturates and benzodiazepines) need to be reduced slowly rather than suddenly. Stopping these drugs suddenly may produce extra and more severe symptoms. If barbiturates are stopped suddenly, for example, fits can occur.

6. No addict should 'withdraw' alone. An addict who is 'kicking' a habit needs support and encouragement. Obviously, the amount of support an addict needs depends on the nature of his addiction. A tobacco addict will probably only need sympathy and understanding. A benzodiazepine addict will need much more help.

7. While going through the withdrawal period, addicts may become mentally disturbed and severely depressed. This phase is usually only temporary but it must be expected.

8. Any unusual or worrying symptoms which occur during withdrawal should be reported to the patient's general practitioner as soon as possible.

9. In some areas doctors will have access to hospital or specialist facilities for addicts wishing to give up their addictions. When these facilities are available they should be used. In many areas, however, addicts will have to withdraw at home.

10. Addicts going through withdrawal will probably have to be reminded to eat and drink. They will need supplies of both food and drink made available for them.

11. It is a waste of time allowing an addict to go through the agony of a withdrawal unless something is done to improve his personal circumstances – and to help eradicate the pressures and problems which led to the need for drugs in the first place.

SOURCES OF HELP

There are now hundreds of national and local self-help groups in existence. Below I have listed the names and addresses of the larger and most important organisations. By contacting these centres you should be able to obtain the names and addresses of local organisers and times and places where local groups meet.

I have not included the names and addresses of smaller, local groups since these change far too regularly for a book to be able to provide useful, up-to-date information. You can get the names and addresses of local associations by looking in your telephone directory, by consulting your own general practitioner (or by looking on the notice board in his waiting room or talking to his receptionist), or by visiting your local library. Libraries are frequently underestimated as sources of information of this type but most can provide a comprehensive list of all local organisations offering advice, help and support. Look in the reference section and ask for the information you require if it is not instantly available.

NATIONAL ADDRESSES

Alcohol

Alcoholics Anonymous PO Box 514, 11 Redcliffe Gardens, London SW10 9BQ Tel: 01–352–9779

Al Anon Family Groups (help and advice for families and relatives) 61 Great Dover St, London SE1 4YF Tel: 01–403–0888

Drinkwatchers (advice for people who think they are drinking too much) Accept Services UK, 200 Seagrave Rd, London SW6 1RQ Tel: 01–381–3157

Alcoholics Anonymous has a large network of local organisations and publishes an excellent range of leaflets. For more information about problems related to alcohol I suggest that you contact them.

Drugs and solvents

There are scores of organisations and associations which were formed to provide help and support for drug addicts and their relatives. Unfortunately, there are no organisations with a complete national network of local groups. For the names and addresses of local groups I suggest that you consult the telephone directory, your own general practitioner, the local library or your nearest independent local radio station. Or you could contact:

SCODA (Standing Conference on Drug Abuse) 1/4 Hatton Place, Hatton Garden, London EC1N 8ND Tel: 01–430–2341

Tranquilliser users will find background information and practical advice in my book *Life Without Tranquillisers* (Piatkus Books, £6.95; and in paperback by Corgi Books).

Food

Overeaters Anonymous (advice, help and support) 1 Oxford Court, Warwick Rd, New Barnet, Herts

Food Allergy Association (advice for food allergy sufferers & relatives) 27 Ferringham Lane, Ferring, West Sussex BN1 5NB

Slimmer Silhouette (national network of slimming clubs) 21 Rolle St, Exmouth, Devon EX8 1HA

Gambling

Gamblers Anonymous 17/23 Blantyre Street, Cheyne Walk, London SW10 Tel: 01–352–3060

GLOSSARY

Acapulco gold: type of marijuana, grown in Acapulco
acid: LSD
acid head: LSD user
action: buying drugs
amphetamine: type of central nervous stimulant
angel dust: PCP or phencyclidine
antidepressant: drug that elevates the mood
anti-freeze: heroin

Babysitter: someone caring for a drug user on a 'trip'
bagman: drug supplier
bang: the thrill that using drugs produces
barbiturate: type of depressant, sleep inducing drug that produces intoxicant-like effects
bennies: amphetamines
benzodiazepine: type of tranquilliser
Bernice: cocaine
bhang: type of cannabis
black beauty: amphetamine
blow: to inhale a drug
blow cocaine: to snort cocaine
blow horse: to sniff heroin
blue birds: barbiturates
blue devils: barbiturates

blue heaven: barbiturates
Bombay black: type of cannabis
booze: alcohol
boy: heroin
brewing up: preparing for injection
buttons: mescaline
buzz: drug effect

C: cocaine
cancer stick: cigarette
candy: barbiturates
candyman: drug dealer (particularly in cocaine)
cartwheels: amphetamines
chasing the dragon: burning heroin on silver paper and inhaling the vapour
chipping: using drugs occasionally
Christmas trees: amphetamines
clean: abstinence from drugs
cold turkey: giving up a drug suddenly, usually involuntarily
coming down: gradual disappearance of drug effect
contact: drug dealer
copilots: amphetamines
crash: to sleep under drug influence
crashing out: gradual loss of consciousness, or disappearance of drug effect

cross tolerance: the use of an alternative drug to help relieve the withdrawal symptoms caused by a drug on which a patient is addicted

cubes: LSD

cut: adulteration or dilution of a drug

Dealer: someone who sells drugs

dealing: buying drugs

dependent: attempts used to be made to differentiate between 'dependence' and 'addiction' but today the two words are used synonymously

detoxification: getting rid of the toxic properties of a substance

diconal: synthetic narcotic

dike: diconal

dolly: methadone

dope: cannabis

downers: depressants and sedatives

Fag: cigarette

fix: a dose of a drug

fixing: injecting straight into a vein

flake: cocaine

flashback: hallucinatory effects that occur long after a drug has been used

footballs: amphetamines

freaks: addicts

freebase: method of using cocaine that involves heating the drug

Gear: syringe, needle etc for injection

girl: cocaine

gold dust: cocaine

goof balls: barbiturates

grass: cannabis

Habituation: attempts used to be made to differentiate between 'dependence' and 'habituation' but today the two words are used synonymously

hallucinogen: a drug that alters moods and behaviour but particularly perception

happy dust: cocaine

harry: heroin

hash: cannabis

hashish: cannabis

hearts: amphetamines

hemp: cannabis

hepatitis: a liver infection often caused by the use of non-sterile needles

high: drug effect

hit: drug effect

holding: possession of drugs

hooked: addicted

horrors: hallucinations

horse: heroin

hustling: buying drugs

Indian hemp: cannabis

J: joint or marijuana cigarette

jones: heroin habit

joy powder: heroin

juice: alcohol

junk: heroin

junkies: heroin addicts

Kicking: withdrawing from drug dependence

Leapers: amphetamines

lid proppers: amphetamines

lines: cocaine

LSD: lysergic acid diethylamide

lucy in the sky with diamonds: LSD

Magic mushroom: psilocybin

mainlining: injecting straight into a vein

marijuana: cannabis

mary jane: cannabis

mescaline: a type of hallucinogen

mesc: mescaline

methamphetamines: stimulants of the amphetamines type

methedrine: a type of methamphetamine usually known as 'speed'
Mexican brown: a type of cannabis
Mexican mud: a crude opium
miss emma: morphine
mixed addiction: when an addict is hooked on several drugs – eg cocaine and heroin
mule: a drug courier
mumbling: tricking a doctor into prescribing

Nail: cigarette
narcotic drugs: drugs that are central nervous system depressants
nickel bag: five dollar bag of heroin

Opiates: narcotic drugs derived from the opium poppy plant
over-the-counter drugs: drugs available without a prescription

Pep pills: amphetamines
peyote: natural hallucinogenic substance found in a type of cactus (also known as mescaline)
pinks: amphetamines
pop: to inject drugs under the skin rather than in a vein
pot: cannabis
potentiation: when two drugs are taken together and one strengthens the action of the other
psychoactive drug: one that has an effect on the mind, influencing mood or behaviour
push: to sell drugs
pusher: dealer

Reds: barbiturates
reefer: cannabis cigarette
roach: a long pin that can be inserted into a cannabis cigarette so that it can be smoked right down to the butt

run: daily use of drug

Sacred mushroom: psilocybin
sauce: alcohol
scag: heroin
scat: heroin
scoring: obtaining drugs illegally
script: drug prescription
sedative: a drug that produces sleep
set of works: needle, syringe etc for injecting
shake: to break a drug habit
shit: just about any type of drug
shooting up: injecting
skin popping: injecting a drug directly into the skin
sleepers: barbiturates
smack: heroin
smoke: cigarette
snort: method of using cocaine by sniffing
snow: cocaine
snowbird: cocaine
snowbirds: cocaine addicts
speed: amphetamines
speedball: mixture of cocaine and heroin
spike: needle, syringe etc for injecting
star dust: cocaine
stick: cannabis
stimulant: a drug that stimulates or excites the central nervous system
stoned: under the influence of drugs
super flu: heroin withdrawal symptoms
synergism: when two drugs combine together to produce a greater effect than each drug would produce if taken alone
synthetic: man-made rather than occurring naturally

£10 bag: heroin
tea: cannabis
thai stick: cannabis

tracks: needle scars

tranquilliser: central nervous system depressant that is used to calm tensed individuals

tranx: tranquillisers (usually benzodiazepines)

trip: drug effect

Uppers: amphetamines

ups: amphetamines

Volatile solvent: substance that can easily be vaporised and sniffed to obtain an intoxicant effect

Wake ups: amphetamines

weed: cannabis

white stuff: heroin

withdrawal syndrome: physical and mental symptoms that result from stopping a drug that has been taken for some time

Yellow jackets: barbiturates

yellows: barbiturates

INDEX

The College of West Anglia

Tennyson Avenue • King's Lynn • PE30 2QW • Tel: (01553) 815306

LEARNING *Resource Centre*

• Library • IT • Media Services •

The card holder is responsible for the return of this book
Fines will be charged on ALL late items